PHILIPPINES

BY MARY CAMPBELL WILD

**LUCENT
BOOKS ®**

THOMSON
★
™
GALE

San Diego • Detroit • New York • San Francisco • Cleveland • New Haven, Conn. • Waterville, Maine • London • Munich

© 2004 by Lucent Books. Lucent Books is an imprint of The Gale Group, Inc.,
a division of Thomson Learning, Inc.

Lucent Books® and Thomson Learning™ are trademarks used herein under license.

For more information, contact
Lucent Books
27500 Drake Rd.
Farmington Hills, MI 48331-3535
Or you can visit our Internet site at http://www.gale.com

LIBRARY OF CONGRESS CATALOGING-IN-PUBLICATION DATA

Wild, Mary Campbell.
  Philippines / by Mary Campbell, Wild.
p. cm. — (Modern nations of the world)
Summary: Presents information on the history, geography, people, culture, historical
struggles, and contemporary issues of the Philippines.
Includes bibliographical references and index.
  ISBN 1-59018-120-4 (hardcover : alk. paper)
  1. Philippines—Juvenile Literature. [1. Philippines.] I. Title. II. Series.
DS655.3 .W55 2004
959.9—dc21

2003011141

Printed in the United States of America

CONTENTS

INTRODUCTION

A BEAUTIFUL LAND, A VOLATILE LAND

Young boys ride a water buffalo across a field at the base of Mount Mayon, one of the world's most explosive volcanoes.

Mount Mayon is an apt symbol of the Philippines. It is a breathtakingly beautiful volcano favored by photographers because of its picture-perfect cone. However, Mount Mayon is also one of the most volatile volcanoes on earth. Like their photogenic volcano, the 7,107 islands that make up the Philippines are also beautiful but volatile. They sit on the Ring of Fire, a rim of volcanoes that arc along the Pacific Ocean. This precarious position on the Ring of Fire makes the landscape and seascape extremely unstable. Volcanoes and earthquakes, as well as typhoons and monsoons, are a part of the geography, the culture, and the economy. It is a land frequently ravaged by the same forces of nature that are the source of its great physical beauty and abundant resources.

Through the centuries, the Philippine Islands have been invaded by fortune seekers as well as by nature, and this has caused a second kind of volatility. As part of Southeast Asia, the Philippines lies at an easily reached point between East and West, making it a cultural crossroads. From earliest times, the region has attracted outsiders. The islands were visited by Chinese traders, anxious to sell goods from their nearby homeland; by Arabs who introduced Islam, which remains a viable force in the south; Spanish colonizers who during their three-hundred-year reign established Catholicism and a landed gentry; and most recently by Americans who during their fifty-year rule introduced a public education system and a democratic system of government.

Because of its physical makeup and colonial influences, the Philippines is a nation characterized by diversity, stark contrasts, and opposing forces. Its people are physically separated by the islands they live on; even those who inhabit the same island are frequently separated from one another by high mountain ranges. Filipinos speak different dialects and practice different customs. The vast majority are Christians, but many of them also retain animist beliefs. A small minority are Muslim, but they make their voices heard and are fiercely protective of their land. It is a country that has struggled to keep its rich cultural heritage throughout a history of dependency on foreign conquerors.

Many of the country's present problems can be traced to its colonial past, when the Spanish colonizers offered land in exchange for loyalty. An enormous disparity in wealth and power between a small group of affluent Filipinos and the great majority of impoverished people continues to be a source of tension and instability. The favoritism afforded to the elite ruling class has caused the political environment to be as unstable as the physical one. Governmental corruption has led to two people's revolutions since 1986. The turmoil has prevented the country from strengthening its economy, which is subject not only to the vagaries of nature but to the investment interests of a global community wary of the Philippines' volatile political climate.

As the Philippines searches for a way to stabilize in the coming decades, its number one roadblock to success is a poverty that is fed by nature's fury, by an eagerness to shed the cloak of a colonial past, and by political upheaval. The country's best hope for a bright future remains the resourcefulness and resilience of the people, the stewards of a magnificent landscape.

1

ISLAND GEMS ON A RING OF FIRE

From the air, the Philippines is a breathtaking array of emerald islands floating in sapphire seas. This picture of tranquility is somewhat deceiving. The archipelago of more than seventy-one hundred islands is one of the most beautiful places in the world, but it is also one of the most volatile. Millions of years ago, an earthshaking clash of tectonic plates occurred deep beneath ancient oceans. The billions of tons of molten ash fired from an opening in these opposing plates forged the Philippine Islands. These islands sit precariously on top of what is called the Ring of Fire. Stretching over thirty thousand miles around the rim of the Pacific Ocean, the ring contains more than 75 percent of all the active volcanoes in the world. The Philippines contains about one hundred volcanoes, and nearly two dozen of these are considered active. These volcanoes, often accompanied by violent earthquakes and tsunamis, are responsible for almost indescribable destruction. They are also the reason for a lush landscape, a fertile soil, and a people who live with an unrelenting truth—that the forces of nature constantly redefine the bountiful land on which they live.

LOCATION

It would be hard to understand Filipinos without first understanding their unique physical setting. They live on islands that are midway between the East and the West, that are narrow and volcanic, that are visited yearly by monsoons and typhoons, and that are surrounded by a deep sea teeming with life.

The Philippine Islands are located north of the equator in the western Pacific Ocean. Officially part of Southeast Asia, the Philippines stretches for about 1,150 miles from a point near the southern tip of Taiwan to a point near the northern tip of Borneo. Its coastline measures 22,550 miles, about twice the length of the shoreline of the United States.

Taken together, the landmass of the islands is relatively small—about 115,000 square miles. That is roughly the size of Arizona or about two-thirds the size of the Philippines' first colonizer, Spain. All of the land is bordered by various parts of the Pacific Ocean: the South China Sea to the west, the Bashi Channel to the north, the Philippine Sea to the east, and the Sulu and Celebes Seas to the south.

MAIN DIVISIONS OF LAND

The people of the Philippines, called Filipinos, have an often-told creation myth to explain their precarious existence in a watery world. In a time when only the sea and the sky existed, the story goes, a weary bird was desperately searching for a place to roost. He cleverly started a quarrel between the sea and the sky. The angry sky hurled boulders into the sea. The sea fought back with huge, crashing waves. Eventually, the sky won the battle, and the boulders it threw down into the sea formed the Philippines—the first land on Earth.

Many of the Philippine Islands are tiny collections of coral not much bigger than those fabled boulders. Although there are officially 7,107 islands, most of them are small. Eleven islands make up about 95 percent of the total land area. Filipinos have only named 2,773 of their islands and inhabit only about a thousand of them.

The Philippines consists of more than 7,100 islands like these that sit atop active underwater volcanoes.

Underwater eruptions and stormy seas constantly redefine the Philippines, but there are three major geographic divisions: Luzon, Mindanao, and, sandwiched between them, a collection of islands called the Visayas. Luzon, the largest and most populated of the islands, is the site of Manila, the capital of the Philippines and its busiest port. Manila lies on the eastern coast of Manila Bay, one of Asia's best harbors. The Luzon division also includes Mindoro, the seventh largest island in the Philippines.

Mindanao, the second largest island, is the home of 9,692-foot-high Mount Apo, the Philippines' tallest volcano, sometimes called the grandfather of the Philippine mountains. The

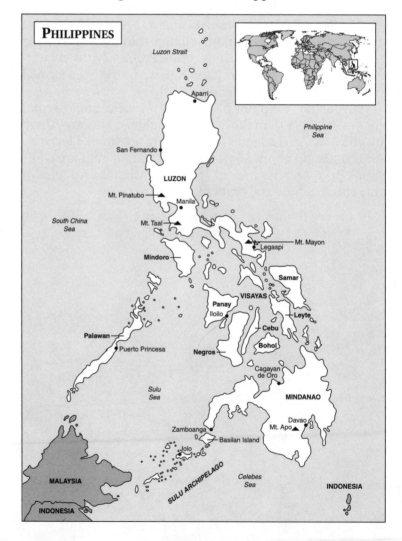

THE CHOCOLATE HILLS

The oval-shaped island of Bohol in the central Visayas has some of the most unique terrain in the Philippines. The name *Bohol* is from the word *boho*, meaning "hole," probably because the island's limestone foundation is riddled with caves: an average of thirty in each of its forty-seven towns. The most unusual and visible land formations on Bohol, however, are the Chocolate Hills. There are more than twelve hundred of these uniformly shaped structures, which have evolved over millions of years. With a little imagination, these mysterious rock formations can be viewed as enormous chocolate candies when their grassy slopes turn brown in summer. Filipino legend describes the symmetrical rock formations another way—as the tears of a giant who once cried over a lost love.

only recorded eruption was in 1640, but volcanic activity deep within its core continues to be detected. The port of Davao is the main city on this island and the hub of commerce in the southern Mindanao region. Zamboanga is another important port. To the east of Mindanao is one of the best-known ocean trenches in the world, the Mindanao Deep, also called the Philippine Trench. The bottom is seven miles below the ocean's surface, a depth that exceeds the altitude of Mount Everest.

About six thousand islands compose the Visayas, but most are tiny and sparsely populated. Six large islands dominate the Visayas. The most important is Cebu, located in the central Visayas. Cebu is historically significant because it is the island where Spanish explorer Ferdinand Magellan first landed in 1521. Its capital of the same name is also the region's business and industrial center, surpassed only by Manila in cosmopolitan atmosphere and dense population (1.6 million). The island of Cebu has a deepwater port and is connected by bridge to an international airport on the tiny island of Mactan, making it attractive to both Filipino and foreign investors. Nearby Bohol is best known for its Chocolate Hills, but it is also one of the nation's largest coconut-growing areas. In the eastern Visayas, Samar and Leyte are rich in natural resources, including fertile acres of untouched forestland and abundant marine life. In the western Visayas, Negros continues to be the sugar capital of the Philippines, a commercial enterprise that has its roots in Spanish colonial times. Panay boasts the most important port in the western region, a port that was opened to international shipping in 1855.

The third largest of the Philippine islands, Palawan, is a finger-shaped sliver of land situated west of the Visayas between Mindoro and North Borneo. Palawan is a sanctuary for fauna and flora found nowhere else in the world. Many species more closely resemble those of Borneo than those of the rest of the Philippines, suggesting that during the last ice age, land bridges connected Palawan to Borneo. Palawan is also known for its black marble caves and for the Tabon Caves, an archaeological site where human remains dating back at least twenty-two thousand years were discovered.

At the tip of Mindanao's Zamboanga Peninsula lies the island of Basilan and to Basilan's southwest is the Sulu Archipelago, a string of tiny volcanic islands and coral islets that stretch like gemstones almost to Borneo. Jolo, the walled capital of Sulu Province, was the first Muslim sultanate in the Philippines and has been a center of trade since the fourteenth century.

TERRAIN

Although there are dramatic differences between islands in this complex country, one common geographic characteristic is mountainous terrain. About 65 percent of the land area is mountainous, with ranges running north to south through the archipelago. On the large islands, the mountain ranges form a rugged interior, called the uplands, which rise from three thousand to nine thousand feet. The large islands feature mountain ranges with plains sandwiched between and coastal lowlands where the soil is the most fertile and where consequently most of the population lives. Smaller islands often have heavily forested mountainous spines with narrow coastal lowlands.

Luzon has the Philippines' highest and most rugged mountain ranges. The Sierra Madre, the longest mountain range, runs along the eastern side of Luzon. The Cordillera Central, the highest and largest mountain range in the Philippines, covers more than seven thousand square miles of Luzon. These ranges shelter the agriculturally important Cagayan River Valley from the ravages of typhoons.

Although the numerous bays, gulfs, and harbors carved out by a long and irregular coastline are the Philippines' most notable and economically significant bodies of water, the islands do have important inland rivers, lakes, and waterfalls. The Cagayan River in northeastern Luzon is the longest in the Philippines. The Pampanga and Agno Rivers on Luzon and the Agusan and Pulangi (Rio Grande) Rivers on Mindanao are important sources of hydroelectric power. The Pasig River is short—ten miles—but strategic: The capital city of Manila is situated at its mouth. The Pasig empties into heart-shaped Laguna de Bay, the Philippines' largest fresh-water lake. Pagsanjan Falls on Luzon and Limunsudan Falls on Mindanao are two of the country's most spectacular wa-terfalls.

The deep waters of the Philippines' volcanic seascape pro-vide vast jewel-like gardens of coral that teem with brightly colored tropical fish. Two of the most famous are the Apo Reef, located twenty nautical miles off the west coast of Min-doro, and the Tubbataha Reefs in the Sulu Sea, near Palawan. Although rough seas, especially during the typhoon season, make the Tubbataha Reefs difficult to visit even for the most experienced divers, the Philippine government has desig-nated fifty-six thousand acres of this surreal underwater ter-ritory as a national marine park.

VOLCANOES

Living in the shadow of active volcanoes and dealing with the aftermath of their eruptions is a way of life in the Philippines. Volcanologists at the University of North Dakota concluded that

the volcanoes of the Philippines are the most deadly and costly in the world. Fatalities have been caused by 13% of the historic eruptions, most notably at Taal and Mayon, and 22% of the eruptions caused damage. Mud-flows are more common in the Philippines, compared to other regions, because of heavy rains. Tsunami are more commonly associated with eruptions in the Philippines than in any other volcanic region.[1]

Three of the Philip-pines' most feared volca-noes overshadow the Luzon landscape. At 1,312 feet, Taal, just thirty miles south of Manila, is

Active volcanoes and the destruction they cause are a central part of life in the Philippines.

small by volcanic standards, but it is lethal. The second most active volcano in the Philippines, it has erupted more than forty times in the last five hundred years. Because of its un-usual location in the center of Lake Taal, which itself is the crater of a prehistoric volcano, it is sometimes called "the vol-cano within a volcano." One of the main sources of informa-tion regarding early eruptions of Taal is a small book called *The Eruption of Taal Volcano, January 30, 1911,* by Father Miguel Saderra Maso, published in 1991. In this book, Maso includes translations of eyewitness accounts of Taal's erup-tions dating back to the sixteenth century. He includes this graphic description of an eruption on September 24, 1716:

> Great masses of smoke, water, and ashes rushed out of the lake, high up into the air, looking like towers. Si-multaneously there was a great commotion in the earth which stirred up the water in the lake, forming im-mense waves which lashed the shores as though a vio-lent typhoon were raging. . . . This eruption killed all the fishes, large and small, the waves casting them ashore in a state as if they had been cooked, since the water had been heated to a degree that it appeared to have been taken from a boiling caldron.[2]

The most violent of Taal's recorded eruptions was in 1911. Taal spewed boulders, sand, lava, mud, ash, and sulfuric acid over a wide area, killing more than thirteen hundred farm-ers and fishermen. Taal's last violent eruption was in 1965, but seismic shudders continue to rock the earth beneath Taal, and it continues to make the top ten list of the world's deadliest volcanoes.

Mayon, located in southeastern Luzon in the Bicol region, is considered the most active volcano in the Philippines. The name *Mayon* is from the Bicol word *magayon,* meaning "beautiful." The volcano's perfectly symmetrical cone shape is frequently featured on posters and in photographs. Mayon is beautiful but dangerous. An eight-thousand-foot-high vol-cano, it has erupted more than forty times in the past four hundred years. The first documented eruption was in 1616, when sailors on a passing Dutch ship witnessed its fury. The second, on July 20, 1766, lasted six days. The most destruc-tive eruption was on February 1, 1814, when three towns were buried in rivers of mud and torrents of ash. The most recent eruption was in the year 2000.

On June 12, 1991, Mount Pinatubo, which lies just north of Manila, awakened after being dormant for about five hundred years. It was the largest volcanic eruption on Earth in more than seventy-five years and one of the most violent in the twentieth century. As is typical of volcanoes along the colliding edges of tectonic plates, Pinatubo did not just erupt, it exploded. Before June 12, 1991, Pinatubo rose about 5,725 feet above sea level. Today, it is considerably shorter because almost five hundred feet of the volcano were blasted away by the cataclysmic event that fired rock, lava, and ash as high as twenty-two miles into the air. Avalanches of hot ash (pyroclastic flows) poured down the slopes and filled surrounding valleys with layers of debris as deep as six hundred feet. Enormous rock- and ash-laden rivers of mud, called lahars, engulfed towns and covered acres of some of the best rice-growing land. Lahars continue to be a threat in the area because of the 1991 eruption.

BALMY WEATHER WITH A TWIST

The Philippines' position just north of the equator places it in the tropics, where the climate is warm and humid year-round. The average mean temperature is 81° F. The coolest month is January, and the warmest month is May. Weather patterns are complex, but they can be roughly divided into three basic seasons: a rainy season from June to October; a cool, dry season from November to February; and a hot, shorter, dry season from March to May.

During the summer monsoon season, from June to October, prevailing winds blow from the southwest. They bring with them drenching rains that replenish the land after the dry season, restoring its emerald appearance. However, monsoons also cause flooding, particularly since they are not the only source of stormy weather during those months. The Philippines lie on a typhoon belt, which puts the islands in the path of dangerous storms and often deals a double punch of precipitation: monsoons and typhoons. Typhoons are characterized by strong winds that spin in a counterclockwise motion, generating high waves that erode the coastlines and threaten the existence of the smallest islands. Typhoons pose a particular threat to northern and eastern Luzon, the Bicol region of Luzon, Mindanao, and the eastern Visayas.

AGRICULTURE

Despite its mountainous terrain and fickle weather, the Philippines is essentially an agricultural country. About 47

MOUNT PINATUBO

Before it violently erupted in 1991, about 1 million people lived within thirty miles of Mount Pinatubo. They included thousands of Filipino villagers and about twenty thousand American military personnel and their families at Clark Air Base and Subic Bay Naval Station. Despite the great number of people who were at risk, only about 250 Filipino low-landers and twenty of the twenty thousand Aeta villagers living on the slopes died as a result of the powerful eruption.

This was not due to luck. It was the result of the joint efforts of a team of specialists from the U.S. Geological Survey (USGS) and the Philippine Institute of Volcanology and Seismology (PHIVOLCS). Scientists know of no way to stop a volcano from erupting, but they have become adept at determining when it is time to urge people to move out of one's way.

The first signs that Pinatubo was reawakening were a series of small steam-blast explosions that occurred in April 1991. Scientists from PHIVOLCS quickly began on-site monitoring and declared a six-mile-radius danger zone around the volcano. They were joined by USGS scientists who brought with them specially designed portable instruments to extend the monitoring network on and around Mount Pinatubo. For clues to its future behavior, the team also studied the volcano's violent past. When all the data indicated that a huge eruption was imminent, the joint team issued urgent evacuation warnings to the people still living in the volcano's deadly path. Many fled to more distant towns or took shelter in buildings with strong roofs. The USGS/PHIVOLCS team estimate that their forecasts saved at least five thousand lives and perhaps thousands more.

percent of the land is used for growing crops. Volcanic ash, which contains minerals and other nutrients that are beneficial to plants, breaks down quickly and mixes into soil. The nation's farmers make good use of these rich soils found on volcanic flanks and coastal lowlands.

The country's chief crops are rice, corn, coconuts, pineapples, and sugarcane. Rice grows best in the Philippines' four major lowland plains: the Central Plains and Cagayan River Valley on Luzon and the Agusan and Cotabato Valleys on Mindanao. The broad, fertile Cagayan River Valley is the largest rice-growing region in the country. Southern Luzon is also agricultural, but it is narrower and subject to typhoons. Corn is particularly prevalent in the Visayas. Rice and corn are grown throughout the Philippines on numerous tiny farms, primarily to meet family needs. Many farmers also raise root vegetables such as sweet potatoes and cassava, mostly by traditional methods. The farmers depend on the broad-backed carabao, or water buffalo, to plow their fields, and they plant with seasonal weather patterns in mind. However, the government is encouraging farmers to outsmart nature by planting hybrid varieties of rice and corn that are more drought-resistant and that require shorter growing seasons.

The Philippines' major exports are pineapple, sugar, and processed coconut. Coffee and tobacco are also widely grown, mainly for export. Pineapple production remains largely in the hands of foreign corporate interests. For example, two U.S. companies, Dole and Del Monte, operate large pineapple plantations on Mindanao. The Philippines' major export crops were established during its colonial past. Mary Somers Heidhues, an expert on the history and politics of Southeast Asia, writes,

> In the Philippines the Spanish required peasants to grow tobacco for local and international consumption— Manila cigars were a product of this system. Sugar production expanded in areas like the central Philippine islands of Negros and Iloilo. Under American rule, Philippine sugar enjoyed a highly rewarding, protected export market in the USA, although rewards inevitably fell more to landowners and millers than to farmers.[3]

In the case of sugar, what began as a colonial requirement is now a major industry. The Philippines is the world's second largest producer of sugar at more than 2 million tons annually. The Philippine sugar industry employs 556,000 farmers and 25,000 sugar mill workers. Although some sugarcane is grown on Luzon, Negros remains the sugar bowl of

Flooding resulting from monsoons and typhoons is a common occurrence in the Philippines. Here residents of Manila negotiate a flooded street.

the Philippines because the island's western plains support vast sugarcane fields. Unlike rice, corn, and coconuts, sugarcane is usually grown on large farms, called haciendas, as it was when the Philippines was a Spanish colony.

In most of the Philippines' seventy-nine provinces, coconut is a major crop. There are 304 million coconut trees planted nationwide, covering 27 percent of the arable land. The Philippines is the largest supplier of coconut oil in the world, but it is not just the oil that is popular. Filipinos create more than fifty coconut products, including dried coconut meat, called copra, and export more than $800 million worth

Pineapples are one of the country's major exports. Foreign corporations operate most of the Philippines' pineapple plantations.

of such products annually. Coconut meat is sweetened and shredded for baking and is also sold as flour, chips, and candies. Coconut water, a liquid that is removed in making copra, is used to make wine and vinegar. Other parts of the coconut are used in salads, iced desserts and pastries, and preserves. Coconut shells are a valuable commodity because they can be processed into charcoal. Coir, the fiber extracted in the decortication of coconut husks, is used to produce mattresses, brushes, cordage, doormats, erosion control materials, and handicrafts. Coir can even be used as an inexpensive cooking fuel. At home, parts of the coconut tree are used to build the roofs and walls of rural houses.

The Philippines is also the world's largest producer of hemp products. Mindanao grows the most abaca, an inedible plant that is related to the banana. Manila hemp, a tough fiber extracted from the leaves of abaca, is used to make rope and coarse cloth. The papermaking industry in the developed world uses Manila hemp pulp to produce a variety of paper products, from envelopes to teabags. Hemp's relatively short growing period and its versatility could someday allow it to replace timber as a major export, thus protecting the country's rain forests from further decline.

FORESTS

Timber from Philippine forests is a valuable, although dwindling, natural resource. As of 2002, forests and woodlands made up 46 percent of the Philippines, but deforestation as a result of logging operations threatens the existence of many of the country's forests and the ecosystem they support. Large stands of trees still flourish on Palawan and Mindanao, where water-loving hardwood trees called dipterocarps grow as high as two hundred feet in the rain forests. Among the most valuable species are Philippine mahoganies, which were once plentiful in the country's rain forests. In the drier forests that are usually further inland, the most characteristic species is the *molave* which is in the teak family of woods.

About eight thousand kinds of flowering plants grow in the Philippines. Orchids are the most notable of these. More than nine hundred species of orchids grow wild in the Philippine rain forests, and nearly eight hundred of these are native to the islands. The *waling-waling*, a rare orchid with velvety petals tinged in purple, red, and yellow, grows on the slopes of Mount Apo.

MINERALS AND ENERGY

As the country looks for ways to utilize its resources, it has
turned to deep within the earth, where rich mineral deposits are relatively safe from the ravages of nature. The
Philippines' copper and chromite deposits rank among the
largest in the world. There are also large deposits of gold,
silver, nickel, cobalt, iron, coal, gypsum, and sulfur. Gold
mining is common in the Mountain Province of Luzon, on
Masbate in the Visayas, and on Mindanao. Copper, gold,
and nickel are important exports. The Mining Act of 1995
gave the Philippine government more control of mining
operations, but like all modern nations, the country must
weigh possible harm to the environment against boosts to
the economy.

Because of its volcanic landscape and seascape, the
Philippines is the world's second largest producer of geo-
thermally generated electricity. The extremely high temperatures of molten rock (magma) boiling miles below the
earth's surface are the source of the nation's geothermal as-
sets. Geothermal plants generate more than 20 percent of
the national energy supply. In 2002, the Philippines began
to export crude oil to other countries. The first shipment,
from an offshore site near Palawan, went to South Korea.

TREASURES FROM THE SEA

An immense aquatic resource surrounds the Philippines.
The nation's territorial waters, delineated in 1976, encompass two hundred nautical miles and teem with twenty-four
hundred species of fish and mollusks that are a rich source
of both food and income. Commercial fishing in deep waters
accounts for only about one-quarter of the country's catch,
typically large fish such as tuna, salmon, and swordfish.
Most large-scale commercial fishing occurs in deep waters
off the coasts of Palawan, Negros, Mindanao, and Panay.
Close to shore, Filipinos have easy access to smaller fish like
sardines and herring. Even the poorest Filipinos can go out
in small boats and fish for their families. In some of the
small, isolated islands, like those in the Sulu Archipelago,
fishing is the main industry.

Aquaculture—the raising and harvesting of seafood in a
controlled setting—is an important industry, although often
at the expense of the coastal mangrove swamps that are

Many Filipinos living on the more remote islands depend on fishing as a means of subsistence.

cleared to construct the shallow aquaculture ponds. Popular shellfish, such as shrimps and crabs, as well as tilapia and milkfish, are harvested in the ponds and exported.

Despite volcanoes and earthquakes, monsoons and typhoons, the Philippines has attracted migrants, traders, and explorers throughout history. Most were drawn to its shores because of its location and the likelihood of discovering a cornucopia of natural resources. It is easily reached from neighboring countries in Southeast Asia, and it has afforded a strategic outpost for Western nations intent on expanding their interests in the Pacific region. It offers a warm tropical climate and fertile soil, vast mineral deposits, and tracts of valuable hardwood trees. The surrounding seas teem with marine life, and the lengthy coastline is dotted with sheltered bays and harbors. It is easy to understand why those foreign interests who have come to these islands throughout the centuries have wanted to own them.

2 A Nation of Diverse Island Dwellers

If geography is destiny, then the destiny of the Philippines is diversity. Because of its central location in the warm Pacific waters of Southeast Asia, this island nation, stretching 1,150 miles from north to south, has been a magnet for waves of migrants from many places since the earliest times. The influx of people throughout history, who have sometimes intermingled and sometimes sought separate homelands on remoter reaches, has made the Philippines a cultural crossroads. The ethnic and cultural roots of the people who call themselves Filipinos are a unique blend of Negrito, Malay, Chinese, Arab, Spanish, and American influences that took hold through successive invasions.

Early History

Anthropologists believe that nomadic aborigine people called Negritos were first on the Philippine Islands some thirty thousand years ago, and that they crossed on land bridges from mainland Asia during the last ice age. After that, people from the Malay peninsula and from the Indonesian islands arrived. The first waves of the Malay people also walked to the Philippines. Even after the waters rose to bury the land bridges, however, travel by boat from other Southeast Asian territories was relatively easy. The distance from mainland China to the north and from Indonesian islands to the southeast was short, the weather was mild, and numerous islands and atolls provided places to rest along the journey. Later waves of Malays came in boats called *barangays* and settled in scattered communities along the coasts. These settlements were also called *barangays*, just like the seaworthy vessels. By 200 B.C., the Malays had taken over coastal areas, developed a fairly sophisticated agriculturally based society, and displaced the Negritos. As Chester L. Hunt writes in *The Philippines: A Country Study*,

> As the Malays spread throughout the archipelago, two things happened. First, they absorbed, through inter-marriage, most of the Negrito population, although a minority of Negritos remained distinct by retreating to the mountains. Second, they dispersed into separate groups, some of which became relatively isolated in pockets on Mindanao, northern Luzon, and some of the other large islands.[4]

By A.D. 900, the Malay farmers who remained on Luzon were doing business with Chinese traders who had found their way to Luzon and Palawan from nearby Taiwan and the Chinese mainland. Some made the Philippines their home and established trading posts along the coast. Others made regular visits to this newly discovered land of opportunity. By A.D. 1400, Muslim traders and missionaries from Malaya and the Indonesian islands had reached the southern Philippines. The first Muslim sultanate (kingdom) was established on Jolo,

Negritos were the first people to inhabit the Philippines. Here, a modern-day Negrito boy hunts for food.

a small island in the Sulu Archipelago. From there, Islam spread to Mindanao, the Visayas, and southern Luzon. Before Islam could take further hold in the north, however, Spanish conquistadors in search of the Spice Islands arrived in the Visayas in the sixteenth century and began to Christianize the lowland peoples of those islands and of southern Luzon. The indigenous people of the rugged mountains that run the length of the islands, however, remained beyond the Spaniards' reach.

From other parts of Southeast Asia, the coastal areas of the Philippines have always been easy to reach. They have also always been easy to leave. Adding to the mix of a historic influx of outsiders are the physical limits of the habitable islands,

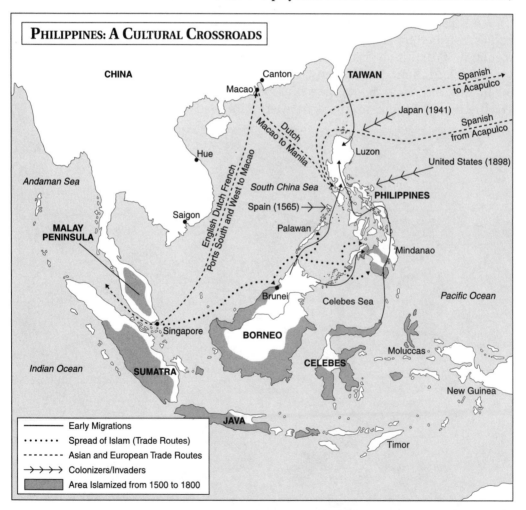

PHILIPPINES: A CULTURAL CROSSROADS

——— Early Migrations
••••••• Spread of Islam (Trade Routes)
------- Asian and European Trade Routes
>>>> Colonizers/Invaders
▓ Area Islamized from 1500 to 1800

many of which are small and volcanic. With the sea beckoning on all sides and with little room to move over on their fertile but limited coastal lands, Filipinos have historically moved off to other islands or up to higher elevations. This trend has continued into modern times.

Categorizing the diverse peoples of the Philippines is a daunting, if not impossible, task. Of a population of nearly 80 million and growing, about 10 percent are considered ethnic or cultural minorities. The continuing migration of peoples has meant eventual interaction among ethnic groups. However, among those isolated on the highest lands or the remotest islands, these interactions remain limited and sometimes hostile, reflecting centuries-old disputes over territory and ideology.

Nowhere is the diverse heritage of the Philippines more evident than in everyday communications. Although Pilipino and English are the official languages, Filipinos speak eleven languages that encompass eighty-seven dialects. When counted in the 1990s, eight of these languages were native tongues for about 90 percent of the population, but mutually incomprehensible dialects within these languages can make communication difficult.

Nearly all lowland rural groups, despite widely varying language and customs, are farmers and fishers; it is only in the degree to which they specialize in one or the other that they differ in livelihood. In the higher elevations, foraging and rice-growing are the primary means of survival. Filipinos are fond of reminding visitors that Manila, the urbanized capital, is not representative of the majority of the Philippines. To grasp the diversity of the Philippines, however, coming to know the people classified as the nation's lowland majorities, for whom Manila is the heart, is a good place to start.

LUZON'S LOWLAND POPULATIONS

The lowland Christians, also known as the Christian Malays, make up more than 90 percent of the population. These groups share Malay roots, live mainly in coastal areas, and reflect Spanish influences, particularly Catholicism, that took strong hold beginning in the sixteenth century. But even within this core population, seven major regional groups with differing dialects, locations, and cultures can be identified.

Of these, the Tagalog are by far the most urbanized, powerful, and largest group. They dominate the economy, the politics, and the culture of the nation. The regional base of the

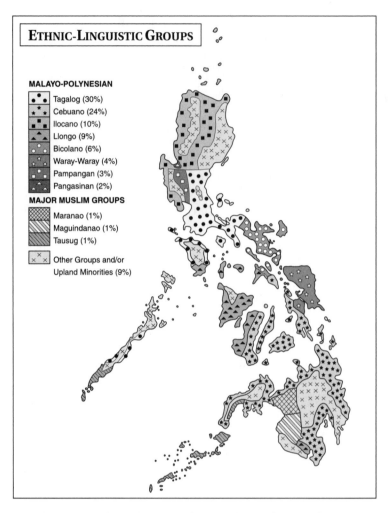

ETHNIC-LINGUISTIC GROUPS

MALAYO-POLYNESIAN
- Tagalog (30%)
- Cebuano (24%)
- Ilocano (10%)
- Llongo (9%)
- Bicolano (6%)
- Waray-Waray (4%)
- Pampangan (3%)
- Pangasinan (2%)

MAJOR MUSLIM GROUPS
- Maranao (1%)
- Maguindanao (1%)
- Tausug (1%)

- Other Groups and/or Upland Minorities (9%)

Tagalog is Manila with a population of 9 million and growing. The official Pilipino language is based on the Tagalog language, a development that has caused some resentment and friction among islanders who speak other dialects.

Three other Christian lowland groups are also based in Luzon: the Ilocano, the Bicolano, and the Pampangan. The Ilocano originally settled along the rocky northern shores of Luzon. Paul Rodell, a specialist in Philippine and Southeast Asian history, traces their more recent movements:

In the past two hundred years, Ilocano people have pioneered new settlements further south of their home base. In the early decades of the twentieth century, they comprised the bulk of Philippine immigrants who

THE MESTIZOS

When discussing the people of the Philippines, mestizos, a Spanish word meaning of mixed blood, is often used. The term refers to two groups: descendants of Spaniards and Filipinos who intermarried *and* descendants of Chinese and Filipinos who intermarried. The Spanish who settled in the Philippines beginning in the sixteenth century frequently married women who were native Filipinos. They called these native women *indias*. Because the Spanish remained the colonizers of the Philippines for more than three hundred years, many present-day Filipinos can claim Spanish-Filipino ancestry.

Mestizos of Chinese-Filipino heritage constitute a much smaller and difficult to define group. The proximity of Taiwan and mainland China to the Philippines encouraged both traders and plunderers to try their fortunes in the Philippines beginning in the ninth century. Some of the men who fought with the legendary Chinese pirate Limahong when he invaded northern Luzon in the sixteenth century reportedly stayed behind and married *indias*, their offspring becoming the first Chinese mestizos. By then, the Chinese community was vital to the welfare of Spain's stronghold in Manila, because Chinese vessels, carrying porcelain, silk, and other exotic wares, were essential to the galleon trade that linked Spanish Mexico with Canton. The Spanish, however, feared that the Chinese merchants would become too numerous and powerful if allowed to roam freely throughout the archipelago, so they forced them to remain in the Parian, a district outside the walls of the Intramuros.

Spain lifted the sanctions when the galleon trade declined, and the Chinese began to settle on lands in northern Luzon, the Visayas Islands, and Mindanao. By the mid-eighteenth century, about a quarter of a million Filipinos were descendants of Chinese merchant fathers and *india* mothers. Revolutionary hero José Rizal, former president Corazon Aquino, and her ally in the People's Revolution, Cardinal Jaime Sin, all claim Chinese ancestry.

The children of this Chinese-Filipino couple will be known as mestizos for their mixed heritage.

worked on sugar plantations and farms in Hawai'i and California. Ilocanos have a reputation for being very hard working and extremely frugal, which undoubtedly results from their difficult life on their ancestral farms, that have notoriously poor soil conditions. [5]

The Bicolano live primarily in the southeastern peninsula of Luzon, where volcanic cones dot the landscape and typhoons threaten the livelihood of both farmers and fishers from September to November. Migrations of peoples from both Tagalog and Visayan cultures, plus the isolation of certain inland areas, led to the formation of diverse dialects even among the Bicolano. Close family ties and strong religious values that blend Catholic doctrines and traditional animist beliefs characterize the Bicolano and foster their survival. Large arable tracts of land, varied vegetation, extensive fishing grounds, and rich mineral deposits make up the region's natural wealth. Here, the Bicolano cultivate rice, corn, coconut, abaca, and fruit crops. They also tap the rich mineral deposits of gold, uranium, copper, coal, manganese, and limestone. The seas around the peninsula are among the best fishing grounds in the country, and the Bicolano also make use of them.

Culturally, the Pampangan of central Luzon are worlds apart from their Tagalog neighbors to the east and south. They speak a distinct language (dialect), and that is a source of ethnic pride. The first Pampangan settlers came from Sumatra around seventeen hundred years ago. Finding the area around Manila Bay already occupied, they migrated upriver and established farming communities along the fertile plains bordering the banks of the Rio Chico and Rio Grande de Pampanga. They became known as the dwellers of the riverbanks or Taga-Pangpang. Since the eruption of Mount Pinatubo in 1991, they have also become known as a people who continually battle destructive lahars that threaten their low-lying towns during the rainy season. Because of its strategic location near Manila, Pampanga province has become increasingly industrialized. However, the Pampangan remain primarily an agriculturally based people. They are also renowned as jewelers and goldsmiths, as well as furniture makers and wood-carvers.

VISAYA LOWLANDERS

The people of the Visayas can be divided into three groups. The Ilongo are based in the western Visayas on the islands of

Ilongo musicians from the island of Negros perform at a local marketplace.

Panay and Negros and in southern Mindoro. Their migration to parts of Mindanao has led to friction with local Muslim tribes there. The Cebuano, as their name suggests, are centered on the island of Cebu, the first island to be settled by the Spanish. The Waray-Waray, numbering about 2.4 million, live mainly in the eastern Visayas on the islands of Leyte and Samar. These three regional groups differ linguistically from one another, and taken together they also differ in cultural outlook from the lowland peoples of Luzon. Rodell writes:

> The abundant marine resources and rich volcanic soils of the central islands have helped to produce a culture that values music, fun, and gregarious personal relations. A study in contrasts was the marriage of former president Ferdinand Marcos, an Ilocano of simple tastes and conservative personal spending, and his Visayan wife Imelda, whose personal collection of shoes, profligate shopping sprees, and impromptu singing at parties bespoke of her Leyte island origins. The Visayans have well-known local centers of art, especially on Negros Island, where the sugar planter elite have been generous in their support of local musicians, actors, and writers.[6]

UPLAND TRIBAL GROUPS OF THE CORDILLERA

As in America, the immigration and assimilation of diverse populations have led to the characterization of the Philippines as a melting pot. But the Philippines is more like a double boiler, with the lowland peoples occupying the bottom lands while the mountain peoples live separately in the highlands.

Unlike the Christian lowland peoples, the indigenous tribes who live in the mountains of Luzon tend to stay put. They view the land as their sacred domain, bequeathed to them by their ancestors. For them, maintaining their land is not only a means of survival, it is a way of life. The uplanders preserve age-old customs and survive mainly by farming and foraging as their ancestors did. They are artistic and worship spirits that oversee their harvests and protect the well-being of kin. Contrary to the opinion of the government and opportunistic developers, these uplanders view the land, which is typically rich in timber and mineral resources, as their own and well worth fighting for.

In the Cordillera Central mountains, upland tribes can be divided into ten major cultural groups. These tribes vary widely in their degree of technical expertise and in the degree to which they have been exposed to and have accepted lowland cultures. They also differ in dialect; in the way they organize their societies; in they way they express themselves in song, dance, and storytelling; and in their artistic skills such as wood carving and weaving. Despite these differences, they also possess common features that led the Spanish who encountered them to classify them into one great umbrella group, called *Igorrotes*, a Spanish word derived from *Igorot*, a Tagalog word for "people from the mountains." Much to the chagrin of the Spanish, one common feature of the Igorot was a fierce resistance to Christian teachings and acculturation. Unlike the coastal peoples, whom the Spanish conquered rather easily, the Igorot did not undergo Hispanization. Other common traits attributed to Igorot culture are the use of the loincloth for men, ferocity in battle, and full-body tattooing of both men and women in elaborate and symbolic designs.

The Spanish viewed these elusive mountain dwellers as savages, particularly those groups such as the Kalinga and Ifugao, who at that time practiced head-hunting as a way to show superiority over foes. Military assaults by Christians in the lowlands upon the "pagans" in the mountains only served to harden the boundaries between them, and misunderstandings evolved into stereotypes. Maria V. Staniukovich, a Russian anthropologist who lived among the Ifugao, observes:

> In the opposition of "Christian" and "civilized" to "savage" and "wild," still noticeable today, headhunting is the most

THE BANAUE RICE TERRACES

The ideal conditions for growing rice are a warm, humid climate, plenty of water, and flat land. Exactly the opposite conditions exist in the cool, steep Cordillera Central region of northern Luzon. Yet more than two thousand years ago, the indigenous Ifugao people of that region began to carve out the hard, rocky soil of the Banaue Mountains. Using their hands and crude tools, they labored to create terraces where rice could flourish, strategically angled to receive ample amounts of sunlight. The result is an engineering feat and a breathtaking tribute to human resourcefulness that continues to defy nature.

On its website, the International Rice Research Institute (IRRI) reports on the amazing efforts of the Ifugao in a feature titled "Mountains of Rice, Beauty & Toil":

> These peoples have ingeniously created ways to get around the many problems of growing rice in these harsh environments. To emulate the usual conditions for rice-growing, mountainsides have been terraced and complex irrigation systems built to constantly flood the terraced fields. The farmers painstakingly re-inforce the terraces with rocks. They laboriously cut these from boulders or collect them from river bottoms and carry them to the terracing sites. The stones are carefully pitched and fitted to form a wall strong enough to withstand the pressure of the water and mud in the ricefields above. The intricate systems depend on gravity flow from sources far from the fields. The terrace owners cooperate to build and maintain them.

An Ifugao man in traditional dress watches over his rice terraces.

sensational point. . . . During my short stay in Manila, it struck me painfully that the image of "bloodthirsty" Igorot is exploited in modern Philippine mass media (movies, ballet performances, etc.). Needless to say, while with the Ifuago family that adopted me during my field research, as well as while hiking through different areas of Ifugao, I felt much safer than in Manila.[7]

The Ifugao people, who live in the eastern and central Cordillera, are the largest and best known of the Igorot tribes. The Ifugao have strict and elaborate codes of conduct and are the hardworking architects and custodians of the fabled Banaue rice terraces, fields of rice that are tiered up hillsides. Rice dominates their culture as surely as the rice terraces dominate their landscape. Skilled wood-carvers, the Ifugao sculpt sacred figures, the most famous of which are male and female deities called *bulul* that are placed at the entrance of a village storehouse to keep an eye on the precious rice.

The Bontoc, Kankanay, and Ibaloi are also "wet-rice" farmers who, like the Ifugao, have built and maintain sophisticated rice terraces. The Bontoc, centered in the northeastern Cordillera mountains, in the upper Chico River region of Mountain Province, are fairly well known. Part of their fame comes from their unusual custom of hanging their dead in coffins within special burial caves. Bontoc communities are organized around *ato*—small political units or male council houses. The Kankanay and Ibaloi were the most influenced by Spanish and American colonialism and lowland Filipino culture because of extensive gold mines in nearby Benguet that attracted fortune seekers to their area, and because of the proximity of the town of Baguio. Although the Philippines has a tropical climate, mountainous areas can be considerably cooler. And it was for this reason, to escape the heat of Manila's oppressive summer heat, that the U.S. colonial government in its early years cut a steep, winding road along the Cordillera mountains to the town of Baguio, which they established as the summer capital of the country.

The Kalinga and the Tinguian are other peoples who harvest rice in the Cordillera mountains. The lesser-known Isneg, Gaddang, and Ilongot people practice "shifting cultivation," that is, growing a variety of crops in rotation. Finally, the Negrito—descendants of the first inhabitants of the Philippines—formerly dominated the highlands, but by the early 1980s, they were reduced to small groups living in widely scattered locations, primarily along the eastern ranges of the mountains. Many Negrito tribes still face cultural extinction.

Although these landlocked peoples remain isolated from lowland economies, they are not without political clout. In their tenacious resolve to preserve ancient traditions and to protect precious resources, the Igorot have banded together. In 1984, they formed the Cordillera Peoples' Alliance (CPA), a federation of twenty-seven diverse organizations united in the cause of self-preservation.

MUSLIM MINORITIES

Muslim minorities make up about 60 percent of the country's ethnic minorities (which account for only 10 percent of the population). The Muslim are also known as Moros, a name given to them by the Spanish. They live primarily on Mindanao and in the Sulu Archipelago. Linguistically, they can be classified into five major groups. Politically, they are organized into sultanates lead by *datus* and seek recognition as a separate nation. Whereas the cultures of the Igorot reflect a mountainous existence, the cultures of the Muslim minorities of the southernmost provinces of the Philippines reflect a life dominated by water, as can be seen in the names by which they refer to themselves. The Maguindanao, or "people of the flood plain," are the Philippines' largest group of Muslims. They live on Mindanao in the provinces of North and South Cotabato. As their name implies, the waters of rising rivers frequently flood their farmlands, especially during the rainy season when volatile weather patterns are the rule. Also on Mindanao are the Maranao, or "people of the lake." They can be found on the shores of Lake Lanao (also known as Lake Sultan Alonto), which is about twenty-three hundred feet above sea level and is the second largest and deepest lake in the Philippines. The writers of *Insight Guide: Philippines* say of the Maranao: "In cool and aloof isolation they continue to uphold their complex but vigorous sultanate."[8]

The second stronghold of Muslim culture in the Philippines is the remote Sulu Archipelago, a collection of some four hundred volcanic and coral outposts with extensive offshore reefs. Two major ethnic groups, the Tausug and the Samal, inhabit the remote Sulu islands. Most of the Tausug, or "people of the current," live on Jolo, the main island, where the first sultanate was established and Muslim traders and missionaries claimed the first converts to Islam. The Tausug see themselves as the ruling

A mosque on Mindanao rises above a neighborhood of huts. Most Muslims in the Philippines live on Mindanao.

people of the original Sultanate of Jolo and therefore as superior to other groups on the archipelago, possibly the reason they have a reputation for being combative. The second major ethnic group, the Samal, are scattered throughout the Sulu islands, but they also live on the Tawi-Tawi islands, an even more remote chain that extends southward toward Borneo. In both the Sulu and the Tawi-Tawi islands, the Samal live along coasts in compact communities. Their houses are precariously built on stilts and their livelihood is linked to the shallow waters along the islands' shores, where fish literally swim at their feet. In contrast to the Tausug, the Samal are characterized as a very peaceful Muslim group; they claim to have no weaponry. When faced with aggression, the Samal generally take flight, which is fairly easy to do considering their locations.

The Samal live close to the sea; the Bajau, a small but fascinating group, live in houseboats on it. Like the land-dwelling

Samal, the Bajau are a gentle people, who for centuries have lived on the perimeters of more dominant societies, trying to avoid confrontation. Although classified as Muslims, they are far more attuned to the tides and the seasons than to religion. Even today, their nomadic existence on some of the world's most remote seas has won them the name, at least among Westerners, of "sea gypsies."

Anthropologist H. Arlo Nimmo spent a year among the Bajau of Tawi-Tawi documenting their unusual way of life. In his analysis of Bajau society, he describes their watery world:

> To the north and west of the island are the deep waters of the open sea, dotted with rich fishing grounds well-known to Tawi-Tawi's seafaring population. Compared to other seas of the earth, these waters are calm and gentle, but nonetheless, during the seasons of the monsoons only the most hardy venture upon them. To the east and, especially to the south of the island, the seas are shallow and filled with myriad coral islands and reefs which make navigation by large ships virtually impossible. At high tide, the waters are as varicolored as only coral seas can be, but at low tide the great sprawling reefs lie ugly and exposed. It is among these southern reefs and islands that the Tawi-Tawi Bajau have carved their unique ecological niche; their small houseboats ply the waters as regularly and persistently as the fishes themselves.[9]

The Bajau houseboats feature a uniquely designed sail with a "mouth" that enables the boats to go almost directly into the eye of the wind. They are usually made of wood, supplemented with scraps of plastic or other scavenged materials. Twenty square feet of living space may be all that a family has to eat, work, and sleep in.

Although far more at home on the sea than on land, the Bajau do lead a somewhat amphibious existence. At times, they moor their boats on coral reefs and come ashore to trade their wares from the sea for staples such as cassava or to barter for the wood they need to build or repair boats. During the northeast monsoon season, some Bajau moor near the villages of friendly land dwellers and plant rice. After the rice is harvested, however, they return to their home moorages, ready to move again when the time and the tides are right.

Some Bajau never sail farther than the outermost Tawi-Tawi islands; others at one time or another travel the length

THE VANISHING BATAK

The island of Palawan is known for its exotic flora and fauna, many species of which are endangered. At least one of its indigenous peoples faces extinction as well. The forested interior valleys of north-central Palawan Island harbor the Batak, a foraging people with animist beliefs who now number only about three hundred. The Batak are distinguished from other indigenous groups on Palawan by their dark skin and short stature and by their heavy reliance on hunting and gathering of rain forest and riverine resources as means of survival. Often using bows and arrows, they hunt wild pigs and squirrels for food and collect commercially valuable forest products, such as honey, rattan, and Manila copal, a resin produced by the *almaciga* tree that is used to manufacture paint varnish.

The Batak acquire rice, clothing, and other necessities by trading their forest bounty for them. During harvests, they sometimes help lowland farmers to gather crops such as rice, coconuts, or coffee, and adventurous tourists occasionally hire them as guides.

Encroachment on the Batak's forest homes, particularly by lowland settlers, began to surge after World War II, when immigrants from other islands arrived on Palawan.

Traditionally, the Batak's strategy was to retreat deeper into interior forests when threatened. Today, however, the Philippine government has banned further cutting of Palawan's primary forests, and nongovernmental organizations such as the United Tribes of Palawan have pledged their support to the Batak. The goal is to ensure their survival as a people through environmental and legal efforts to protect their land and resources.

of the Sulu Archipelago. In theory at least, vast expanses of calm waters can take them any way the wind blows. It is not just wanderlust, however, that drives the Bajau; their movements coincide with the cycles of the moon, the ebb and flow of the seas, the movement of fish, and the seasons.

Despite their diversity of language, land, and culture, the indigenous peoples of the Philippines share one thing in common: Unlike the population in lowland areas, they are dwindling in numbers, and their land, their livelihoods, and their way of life are threatened by encroachment from outsiders. Speaking on behalf of the Moro and Lumad of Mindanao, historian B.R. Rodil posed the question, "What do the indigenous communities want?" He then responded with an answer that can apply to all of the indigenous populations: "They ask to be recognized as they are, with their distinct cultural identities, with their own traditional territories considered essential to their survival and dignity."[10]

THE FIGHT FOR FREEDOM

For much of its past, the Philippines has been ruled by foreigners who attempted to mold the islands into a colony that would serve their imperialist interests. The longest of these occupations began in the sixteenth century, when Spain laid claim to the islands. The most lasting legacy of the three hundred-year Spanish rule was the Catholic religion, which, since the first baptism took place on the island of Cebu, has shaped the nation's political and cultural life. The Philippines became, and remains, the only Christian nation in Southeast Asia.

THE SPANISH CONQUESTS

In 1521, Ferdinand Magellan, commissioned by Spain to circumnavigate the globe, landed on Cebu and claimed the land for Charles I. One month later, a local chief, Lapu Lapu, killed Magellan in a fierce battle between the Spaniards and the natives on the island of Mactan. The battle was a dramatic

Filipino chief Lapu Lapu prepares to deliver a fatal blow to Spanish conquistador Ferdinand Magellan on the island of Mactan.

foreshadowing of antiforeigner sentiments to come. In far-off Spain, however, leaders were undeterred by Magellan's defeat. In 1565, they sent Miguel López de Legazpi to reclaim the land. Sailing west from a Spanish stronghold in Mexico, Legazpi landed on Cebu. He defeated the local leader and claimed Cebu for Spain, naming it the *Islas Filipinas* or Philippines, in honor of the then-ruling king Philip II.

Spain had two strong motives for establishing a colony in Southeast Asia. The first motive was economic. Spain hoped to find spices like nutmeg growing wild in its new colony. This untapped source of exotic spices, it anticipated, would be as lucrative as that controlled by its archrivals, the Portuguese, who had claimed the Spice Islands in present-day Indonesia. Spain's second motive was religious. Spain was a Catholic country, and its leaders hoped to convert the Filipinos to Catholicism. To achieve this second goal, they relied on a group of Catholic missionaries, referred to collectively as the friars, who accompanied the Spanish conquistadors.

After a few years on Cebu, Legazpi decided that both goals would best be served by relocating his headquarters to Manila, which seemed a natural focal point of the islands. It had an excellent harbor, ample food supplies in the adjoining central Luzon rice lands, and a far larger population of "pagans" to convert to Catholicism.

To further their goals, the Spaniards built numerous government buildings and churches. The most famous construction project they undertook, however, was the Intramuros, or walled city, which faced both the bay and the Pasig River and was the foundation for modern-day Manila. The Intramuros was a well-protected colonial headquarters. The walled city offered protection to a select group of people, however. Only the clergy and the Spanish nobility could live within the Intramuros. The natives, many of whom helped build the city, could not enter its walls except to work as servants.

Spain's hopes of discovering spice-rich lands in the Philippines never materialized. Instead, however, it found that Manila was an excellent port for linking the galleon trade between Asia and Spain's colony of Mexico. Once or twice a year, "Manila galleons" cut through the Pacific waters, exchanging gold and silver from Acapulco on Mexico's west coast for cargoes of silk from China. At the peak of this profitable trade, Manila earned the title "Pearl of the Orient."

SECURING SPANISH AUTHORITY

The Spaniards at first had little interest in venturing into the countryside of Luzon, let alone to neighboring islands. They were content to stay in the Intramuros, grow rich on the profits of the galleon trade, and marry native women. Outside the walls, confined to a district called the Parian, Chinese merchants also profited from and contributed to the galleon trade. As Spain had hoped, this was a prosperous time and, for the

THE FRIAROCRACY

Friarocracy was a term coined by critics of the Catholic clergy's pervasive secular power in the Philippines. There was no separation of church and state in the three hundred years of Spanish rule. From the time that Spain's colonizers set foot in the Philippines, the padres, or priests, were tasked not only with religious conversion but also with firmly establishing the Spanish government's power over the people. According to *Southeast Asia*, published by Time-Life Books:

> Although the Philippines had no spices worth exporting, the five Augustinian friars who accompanied Legazpi found the islands fertile ground for saving souls. For the next three centuries, Spanish friars were to play a decisive role in the unfolding social and economic life of the islands. Not only the Augustinians but . . . the Dominicans, Franciscans, and Jesuits established missions throughout the archipelago, learned to speak the native languages, introduced new crops, such as corn and cocoa from America, and taught the 'civilized' tribes more efficient and productive farming methods.

The friars intentionally did not teach the natives Spanish, which would have allowed their participation in local government.

As a result of their labors and their loyalty to Spain, the friars were given impressive earthly rewards: extensive landholdings, a generous annual subsidy, and perhaps most importantly, positions as the Spanish representatives in local governments. As spiritual guides, town leaders, and political advisers to the Spanish crown, they wielded tremendous power. This power led to abuses, both in the acquiring of wealth and influence and in racism against the *indios*. From Spain's point of view, however, the system worked very well. As a result of the efforts of generations of friars, by 1898 more than 80 percent of the population was Catholic. Only the Muslims in the south and the hard-to-reach tribes in the mountains escaped conversion. As recently as the late nineteenth century, the friars of the Augustinian, Dominican, and Franciscan orders continued to carry out government functions on the local level. Even today, the leaders of the Catholic Church play a powerful role in the workings of government.

most part, a peaceful one. At different times, the Chinese, Dutch, and British navies each tried to seize Manila. However, except for a brief period of British occupation from 1762 to 1764, these attempts to topple the Spanish government failed.

Spain was also highly successful in achieving its second goal: superimposing its religious beliefs on the natives, particularly those in the lowlands. While Manila's population enjoyed prosperity from the galleon trade, Catholic priests, subsidized by the Spanish crown, fanned out over the Luzon countryside to convert the natives. These priests established towns, built around churches, and gave religious instruction to the native population.

Power was sometimes abused, however, and the Spaniards, civilians and clergy alike, often treated the natives unfairly. In the Spaniards' eyes, all people they encountered were uncivilized Indians, or *indios*, just like those they had conquered in Mexico. And the natives were not always receptive to such treatment. Paul Rodell writes:

> The genuine hospitality shown to individual Spanish friars and the nominal acceptance of Spain's authority did not always mean the Filipinos were happy with foreign rule. From 1565 to 1898, there were hundreds of revolts and individual acts of defiance against Iberian [Spanish] rule. The causes of these rebellions ranged from simple anti-foreignism to revenge against individual abusive government officials or friars, to revolt against excessive taxation.[11]

When the galleon trade declined around 1811, Manila's mestizos—the descendants of intermarriages between natives and the Spanish or the Chinese—turned their attention to the fertile countryside. Many of this growing population of mestizos acquired wealth through agricultural ventures such as sugar and hemp growing. Typically, the Spanish mestizos sought ostentatious displays of their wealth, such as building large Spanish-style homes. By the second half of the nineteenth century, they also arranged the best education for their sons, often sending them to Europe. But the pure-blooded Spaniards were wary of this new, affluent class. Paul Rodell notes:

> Many of these new graduates went into business with their families, but many sought careers in the priesthood, an arena jealously guarded by the friar orders. When eventually the new elite attempted to participate in local

political affairs, they often ran afoul of Spanish officials and friars who did not appreciate what they thought was a dangerous and subversive influence. So, despite their obvious upwardly economic mobility, the new mestizo elites found their way stalled by Spanish government officials and religious authorities who clung to power. Even more galling, as the new elites acquired wealth and social standing, these same government and religious officials made racist attacks on their character and abilities.[12]

Regardless of their career plans when they returned home, these young men, referred to as *ilustrados*, meaning "the enlightened ones," had been exposed to more liberal—and liberating—ideas during their stay abroad. As a result, they began to see the possibility of their nation breaking free from Spanish control and ruling itself. Historian James Hamilton-Paterson gives two reasons why the overseas experience fostered a resentment against the colonizers and sharpened the sense of nationalism:

> The first was the developmental gulf between the mother country and her Far Eastern colony that showed only too clearly what a backwater Spain had allowed the Philippines to become. And secondly, those who went to France and Germany and Britain couldn't help noticing how far Spain herself lagged behind northern Europe. They returned to Manila both thoughtful and angry.[13]

THE PHILIPPINE REVOLUTION

As increasing numbers of Filipinos began to question the need for continuing association with Spain, Spain attempted to squelch the opinions of those who questioned its policies. Smoldering nationalist feelings ignited in 1872 when Spanish authorities executed three well-known Filipino priests. They were convicted of "inspiring subversion" after a minor uprising in the province of Cavite near Manila. Fiery reactions followed, and a growing national consciousness began to form. Peasant and *ilustrado* alike saw themselves not as *indios* but as Filipinos, united in a crusade to free their country from the restraints of Spanish rule.

One of the most famous Filipinos to call for reform was a brilliant physician and writer named José Rizal. One of the *ilustrados* sent to Europe to be educated, he penned two novels while there, *Noli Me Tangere* (Touch Me Not) in 1886 and *El Filibusterismo* (The Reign of Greed) in 1891. Both novels contained biting criticisms of Spain's colonial policies in the Philippines and of the so-called friarocracy. In 1892, Rizal returned to the Philippines and founded La Liga Filipina, an organization intent on enacting political reform that would assure equality for Filipinos.

In that same year, a Filipino named Andres Bonifacio founded the Katipunan, a secret revolutionary society. While Rizal focused on change through peaceful means, Bonifacio and the Katipuneros sought independence from Spain by whatever means necessary. Bonifacio founded the Katipunan in Manila, but its message soon spread to the provinces, especially those to the north of Manila, the agricultural heartland of Luzon, where the Filipino elite and the friars owned most of the haciendas and farmlands. There, the laboring native peasants were receptive to Bonifacio's message because they toiled on land that they could not own. At its peak, the Katipunan had some thirty thousand members, both men and women, who were ready for insurrection.

Bonifacio's grassroots movement flourished until betrayed by a Spanish priest on August 19, 1896. Once exposed, the underground movement became an armed and open revolt against Spain. Hundreds of Filipinos were imprisoned and killed in uprisings in and around Manila. The Katipuneros lost battle after battle to the far stronger Spanish military. They also lost their leader. Bonifacio was murdered, not by the Spanish, but by supporters of a rival Katipunan leader, Emilio Aguinaldo.

In December 1896, the Spanish, looking for a way to gain control over the revolution, accused Rizal of insurgency and executed him by firing squad. Rather than quell the dissent, the murder of Rizal, who was by now a hero, only strengthened the national spirit. From a mountainous outpost north of Manila, Aguinaldo and the insurgents formed a rudimentary republican government in 1897 and drafted the Philippines' first constitution. The days of Spanish rule seemed numbered.

AMERICAN INFLUENCE BEGINS

Ironically, Spain's rule in the Philippines ended because of U.S. involvement with Spain's other major colony, Cuba. In April 1898, the United States went to war with Spain over rights to Cuba. As part of their campaign to reduce Spain's global power, U.S. forces destroyed the Spanish fleet in Manila Bay. America needed additional troops to capture Manila, however, and Aguinaldo and his rebels, perceiving the United States as an ally in their struggle against Spain, were happy to provide them. Aguinaldo issued a call to arms that inspired the nation, and soon most of the country was under Filipino control. On June 12, 1898, Aguinaldo declared the Philippines' independence from Spain. The victory, however, was short-lived. Unbeknownst to the fighting Filipinos, Spain and the United States had forged a secret deal in which Spain agreed to be defeated in a battle against U.S. troops in Manila on August 13, 1898. Spain did this to save face, so it would not have to surrender to the *indios*.

The U.S. victory in the Spanish-American War gave the United States the rights to the islands, and Spain ceded the Philippines to the United States for $20 million in the Treaty of Paris on December 10, 1898. Fil-ipinos resented the obvious duplicity that had culminated in the Philippines' becoming a U.S. possession. Furthermore, they resented having had no say in the decision. Historian Donald Seekins, in *The Philippines: A Country Study*, states,

Emilio Aguinaldo was one of the first leaders of a revolutionary society that sought independence for the Philippines.

The Treaty of Paris aroused anger among Filipinos. Re-acting to the $20 million sum paid to Spain, *La Independencia* (Independence), a newspaper published in Manila by a revolutionary, General Antonio Luna, stated that "people are not to be bought and sold like horses and houses. If the aim has been to abolish the traffic in Negroes [referring to the end of slavery in the United States] because it meant the sale of persons, why is there still maintained the sale of countries with inhabitants?[14]

Although the U.S. Congress officially declared the Philippines a colony as a result of the Treaty of Paris, tension, ill-will, and fighting continued between American and Filipino forces. A war of resistance against U.S. rule, led by Aguinaldo, broke out in 1899 and continued until 1902. Although Americans initially used the term "Philippine Insurrection" to refer to the hostilities, Filipinos and an increasing number of American historians now refer to it as the Philippine-American War. Aguinaldo was captured during this war and ultimately swore allegiance to the United States. Resistance to U.S. rule then gradually died out.

Unlike the Spanish, the Americans encouraged Filipinos to be involved in their own political affairs. However, the Americans wanted Filipinos to model their emerging nation after the United States. First, U.S. officials introduced a democratic form of government based on that of the United States and trained Filipinos to be its civil servants. Second, the Americans established a public education system that was open to all Filipinos. Instruction was offered in English, further promoting assimilation of American ideals and culture.

Despite an infusion of the American way of life, however, nationalist interests remained strong, and eventually the lob-

THE MARCH ON BATAAN

After Japanese forces overtook Manila during World War II, they fought their way down the Bataan Peninsula. General Douglas MacArthur, who was in charge of the Allied forces, commanded his troops on Bataan from his headquarters on the fortress island of Corregidor. When the Japanese stormed Corregidor in 1942, MacArthur fled to Australia, issuing his famous promise, "I shall return." The United States, unable to send reinforcements, left Filipino and U.S. soldiers defenseless. The outcome was a gruesome part of Filipino as well as U.S. history. The Japanese captured nearly eighty thousand prisoners on the Bataan Peninsula and forced them to march along its eastern coast to prison camps about sixty miles to the north. Many soldiers were already ill and weak from lack of food and water. To add to their misery, the walk took place in April under a blistering sun. Estimates are that as many as ten thousand soldiers, treated harshly by their enemy, died on the way. Among those taken as prisoners of war was the man who was later to become the controversial president of the Philippines—Ferdinand Marcos. Marcos, like many survivors of the march on Bataan, joined guerrilla forces in the mountains of Luzon, attacking the Japanese troops until 1944, when MacArthur made good on his vow to return.

bying efforts of Philippine legislators resulted in the passage of the Tydings-McDuffie Act by the U.S. Congress. Under its provisions, a commonwealth government was formed in the Philippines in 1935, Manuel Quezon was elected president, and independence was scheduled for 1946. The 1935 constitution gave Filipinos considerable, but not total, control over their country. The United States still determined the foreign policies of the commonwealth, including tariff agreements. Wealth remained in the hands of the mestizo elite, who established firm ties with the country's newest foreign ruler.

WORLD WAR II AND THE JAPANESE INVASION

Within a few years of the commonwealth's inception, however, the Philippines' tortuous path to nationhood met another barrier that was beyond its control. This time it was the advent of World War II. In 1941, ten hours after attacking the U.S. fleet at Pearl Harbor, Hawaii, Japanese forces landed on Luzon. They defeated Filipino and American troops in Manila and then conquered the rest of the island. In October 1943, the Japanese declared the Philippines an independent republic, although it was really a puppet republic, and named José Laurel as president. Many of the Philippine elite served under the Japanese, but the Japanese occupation of the Philippines, like the Spanish and American ones before it, heightened most Filipinos' desire for freedom from foreign influence. Underground guerrilla membership reached large-scale proportions. The most powerful of these groups was the Hukbalahap (Huks), a Communist-led organization that consisted primarily of peasants from central Luzon. The word *Hukbalahap* is a contraction of a Tagalog phrase meaning "People's Anti-Japanese Army." The Huks and other guerrilla forces joined U.S. troops returning to the Philippines in 1944 and played a major role in forcing the surrender of the Japanese on September 2, 1945. Still, the liberation of the Philippines took an enormous toll in Filipino lives and property lost.

In accordance with the previous agreement with the United States, Manuel Roxas became the first president of the independent Republic of the Philippines on July 4, 1946. Many issues that emerged during the Japanese occupation remained unresolved, and rebuilding the war-torn country was a daunting task. One major domestic issue was deciding the fate of the collaborators—the Filipinos who had cooperated with the Japanese during the war. Some collaborationist politicians claimed that they had worked with the Japanese to protect the people from the Japanese army, which was known to inflict harsh punishments on rebels. Some nationalists, however, had allied with the Japanese because they believed that the best way to be free at last of Western rule was by establishing solidarity with fellow Asians. And finally, some wealthy landowners had obeyed the Japanese to protect family and personal interests. Not surprisingly, many of the collaborators were the politicians and landowners who resumed their rather feudal control of the Philippines after the war. "The resilience of the prewar elite," historian Donald Seekins observes, "although remarkable, nevertheless had left a bitter residue in the minds of the people. In the first years of the republic, the issue of collaboration became closely entwined with old agrarian grievances and produced violent results."[15]

The "agrarian grievances" powered the Huk Rebellion in 1948. Participants were mainly tenant farmers who now had arms and combat experience. The memory of their landlords' allegiance to the Japanese increased feelings of animosity toward the Filipino elite. In a postwar economy where food and other goods were scarce and land still belonged to the rich, the Huks turned their focus to their own government and launched an armed revolt against it. Although Ramon Magsaysay, elected in 1953, to some extent through U.S. funding, attempted to repress the Huks, they remained a force to contend with through the mid-1960s.

MARCOS AND MARTIAL LAW

It was in this volatile period of peasant unrest, dysfunctional democracy, and a weak economy that a popular congressman from the Ilocano region of Luzon, Ferdinand Marcos, easily won the presidency in 1965. During his first term, the future seemed to brighten for the beleaguered nation. Marcos initiated programs to increase food production, supported land reform initiatives, financed public works projects such as building roads and bridges, and secured economic and military aid from the United States.

Marcos's second term, however, was not as promising. Although he was the nation's first popularly reelected president, not everyone was pleased with his government. Marcos and his flamboyant wife, Imelda, enjoyed an extravagant lifestyle that irked a nation where so many people continued to live in poverty. As he left congress after his State of the Nation address in January 1970, a huge crowd of protesters, most of them students and labor organizers, accosted Marcos. In the countryside, the rural poor, many of them former Huk rebels, were rearming and regrouping as the New People's Army (NPA).

As political tensions heightened, nature also dealt a cruel blow; one of the worst typhoons in the history of the Philippines struck in June, causing widespread devastation and adding to the country's economic woes. It seemed that matters could not get much worse. However, September 1972 brought another blow to the struggling democracy—the declaration of martial law. Historian Rodell writes:

> When Filipinos woke up on the morning of September 21, 1972, they found almost all radio stations silent while television stations broadcast only cartoons. In the evening, President Marcos spoke to the nation announcing that he had issued Proclamation 1081, declaring martial law in response to what he claimed was the threat from Communists and a growing separatist Muslim movement in the south. Initially, Marcos had the support of a sizable portion of the population, which was tired of violent confrontations and worried about armed insurrection and the country's economic future. . . . Still, it was disquieting that the Philippine

Ferdinand Marcos poses with his family during his first term as president of the Philippines. Their lavish lifestyle was greatly frowned upon by the public.

Senate and House of Representatives and all local governments were disbanded and the country's free media and major universities were shut down.[16]

After Marcos replaced the democratic legislature with a parliament that allowed him to assume the role of dictator, three other disturbing patterns emerged. First, Marcos arrested hundreds of well-known critics of his presidency. Among them was Senator Benigno Aquino, a popular politician who many Filipinos felt would be an excellent choice as the next president. Second, businesspeople who supported Marcos were favored for large government contracts, while those who opposed him were often forced out of competition. The term "crony capitalism" became forever linked to the name of Ferdinand Marcos. Third, estrangement between the churches and Marcos grew, as the president's military leaders interpreted religious leaders' efforts to assist the poor as a sign of their Communist sympathies.

Throughout this turmoil, the United States, protecting its commercial and military interests in Southeast Asia, continued to support Marcos. Although few Filipinos were happy with the Marcos government, the catalyst that ignited public fury was the assassination of Aquino at the Manila airport in 1983. Military leaders proposed a "lone gunman" theory, but many Filipinos, rejecting the official story, believed that the government itself was responsible for the murder.

Thousands of people participated in Aquino's funeral procession, said to be the largest gathering in the nation's history. The breadth of the dissent was a clear testimony to the will of the people. Over the next two years, rich and poor alike continued to protest in Manila, and the NPA grew in numbers and military daring in the countryside. Disgust mounted for what was undeniably a corrupt, oppressive, and ineffective regime. As the economy sputtered, the confidence of international investors faltered, and they withdrew their support.

At the urging of the United States, Marcos agreed to hold a "snap election" in February 1986. Marcos did not see this as a risk because he held absolute control over the government and because opposition efforts to support previous alternative candidates had been divided. But this time things were different. This time the name of Corazon Aquino, the widow of Benigno Aquino, was placed on the ballot by an alliance of opposition leaders brought together by the Archbishop of Manila, Cardinal Jaime Sin. More than a million Filipinos

signed petitions supporting her. Thousands of members of the National Movement for Free Elections (NAMFREL) volunteered to stand guard over ballot boxes. Marcos's legislators declared him the winner despite NAMFREL's count, recorded on computer discs, that showed Aquino as the clear victor.

A crowd fills a Manila street during the 1986 People Power Revolution. The revolution toppled Marcos's government.

Election fraud added to civilian unrest, which soon spread to Marcos's own supporters. Marcos's top military leaders abandoned the president, and Cardinal Sin called on the people of Manila to rally to protect the defectors. They did. The resulting four-day nonviolent uprising, known as the People Power Revolution, literally stopped the Marcos regime in its tracks. Describing the drama, historian Rodell writes,

> The popular protest over Marcos's presidency shifted to protecting the dissident military leaders. Hundreds of thousands of people poured into the streets completely halting all traffic by creating roadblocks and setting human barricades. When government tanks and troops advanced, they found old men and women, people in wheelchairs, and nuns praying on their knees.[17]

Corazon Aquino, ignoring Marcos's official inauguration, held a swearing-in ceremony of her own. Marcos finally ceded victory to Aquino and accepted U.S. president Ronald Reagan's offer of safe haven in Hawaii in 1986.

As the 1990s approached, Filipinos were optimistic that the yoke of colonialism, with the corrupt alliances and resentment it had fostered, would at last be shed. Corazon Aquino was elected with the full support of the citizenry, and she promised to turn her full energies to improving the economy and enacting honest government. The luck of the Filipinos seemed to be changing at last.

4

A MODERN NATION EMERGES

The Philippine nation that is emerging in the early twenty-first century is modern in many ways. The literacy rate is high, the economy is recovering and refocusing on industry, the constitution is a blueprint for a democratic republic, and rural areas are far less isolated than in the past. However, sometimes despite the efforts of church, state, and citizens—and sometimes because of them—political and economic turbulence remains the hallmark of the Philippines. When Corazon Aquino was swept into office by a citizens' revolution, the Philippines seemed at last to be a country by the people and for the people. Twenty-five years later, however, Gloria Macapagal-Arroyo would struggle with the same issues that confronted Aquino: how to unite disparate groups to work toward a common cause, how to eradicate poverty, and how to assure her constituents and the world community that the Philippine government was no longer corrupt.

AQUINO AND THE POSTREVOLUTION ERA

Although Corazon Aquino was elected president by popular demand, not everyone was on her side as she confronted the country's problems. She endured at least six coup attempts during her term as president. Marcos supporters staged the coups. Many still held government jobs or were dissident military leaders opposed to returning the nation to civilian control. There were also continuous uprisings among leftists, those either directly or indirectly affiliated with the Communist Party of the Philippines, who clamored for agrarian reform.

Although Aquino introduced a number of social and economic reforms and initially was backed by international investors, the economy remained stagnant. Electricity shortages caused almost daily brownouts in Manila and further dwarfed economic growth. The country's treasury was depleted, and the memory of Marcos's corrupt regime lingered.

Once again, turmoil replaced elation over Aquino's dramatic political victory.

The most serious blow to the country's stability, however, was the United States's closing of Clark Air Base after the eruption of nearby Mount Pinatubo. After World War II, the Philippines had granted the United States the right to establish a large number of military bases in the Philippines. The agreement brought an infusion of U.S. money into the economy, but special treatment given to U.S. military personnel (immunity from local laws, for example) galled Filipino nationalists who wanted their former colonial ruler out of their country once and for all. Just as the Philippine senate debated the issue in 1991, Mount Pinatubo erupted, covering Clark Air Base with tons of heavy volcanic ash that crushed hangars and buildings and threatened the safety of its personnel. The result was not only atmospheric but economic fallout. The U.S. military announced that it would withdraw from the site.

On the positive side, throughout Aquino's chaotic six-year term, democracy did survive if not thrive. Aquino's ability to remain in control was partly due to the unwavering loyalty of armed forces chief of staff Fidel Ramos, who

Despite a number of attempts to remove her from power, Corazon Aquino managed to maintain a democratic government.

succeeded her, with her full support, as the next president of the Philippine nation.

RAMOS AND STABILITY, ESTRADA AND SCANDALS

Fidel Ramos was elected president in 1992. He was more successful than his predecessor had been at jump-starting the Philippine economy, partially because the early years of his term coincided with a dramatic growth in the overall Asian economy. Although the collapse of the Asian markets in 1997 did not affect the Philippines as dramatically as it did some neighboring countries, it did cancel out much of the economic progress the country had enjoyed during Ramos's first four years.

In 1998, Ramos's vice president, Joseph Estrada, a movie star turned politician, won the presidency in a landslide election. Much of his support came from the country's poor, who turned out to vote for him in record numbers. Much of his popularity was due to his image as the defender of the downtrodden, a role he played in many of his action movies. Once in office, however, Estrada did very little to alleviate poverty in his country, and the economy again faltered. The Manila stock exchange plummeted while most Asian markets rallied. Negotiations with both Communist and Muslim rebels, initiated by Ramos, collapsed. Estrada's administration was rocked by scandals, among them the discovery that he had been accepting bribes and engaging in tax fraud. Estrada's behavior fell into the category of *garapal*,

Military officers stand guard as Filipinos rally on a Manila street to demand the resignation of President Joseph Estrada.

behavior that is out of bounds, even in a society extremely tol-
erant of malfeasance in government. In November 2000, impeachment proceedings began, but Estrada's supporters
squelched them. For the second time in less than fifteen years,
a firestorm of indignation began to spread.

Estrada was removed from office after a People Power
protest was again orchestrated by Cardinal Jaime Sin and
Corazon Aquino. Citizens in Manila by the hundreds of
thousands took to the streets. This time, there was one notable difference—protesters organized their members by
using cell phone text messages to communicate the details
of where and when to rally.

For all the democratic exercising of rights shown by the
people, many still question the ability of the Philippine nation to ever stabilize. Historian Paul Rodell writes:

> The Philippine president was swiftly deserted by his
> cabinet and the armed forces who joined the "People
> Power II" throngs. The drama ended in a few days when
> the Philippine Supreme Court declared the presidency
> vacant and Vice-President Gloria Macapagal-Arroyo
> was sworn into office. Though pleased with the out-
> come of the recent popular movement, thoughtful Fil-
> ipinos are questioning their culture's political values
> and are seeking a new set of political values that will
> make a future "People Power III" unnecessary.[18]

MACAPAGAL-ARROYO AND DÉJÀ VU

When Gloria Macapagal-Arroyo took the reins of government
in 2001, the nation and the world felt that history was repeat-
ing itself. She was another woman president swept into power
by another people's revolution, another president faced with a
stagnant economy and civil unrest. Despite the country's pen-
chant for revolts and uprisings, she has stated that she does
not fear coups and remains confident that the military fully
supports her. Macapagal-Arroyo's record on solving the country's most serious problems has been impressive. She has introduced more than fifty laws on civil abuses, and her
administration's official Internet website provides a way for
citizens with access to computers to e-mail allegations of
fraud, waste, or mismanagement of government funds.

Macapagal-Arroyo is also credited with renewed efforts to
restore foreign investors' confidence in Philippine markets. She

INFLUENTIAL WOMEN

Three women have made history in the Philippines in recent times. The first, Imelda Marcos, was the controversial wife of President Ferdinand Marcos. Because Imelda Marcos played such a powerful role during her husband's terms of office, their partnership was sometimes called a "conjugal dictatorship." She was born in the Visayas and is said to have never forgotten her roots. In a country beset by poverty, she is perhaps best known as an extravagant international shopper and the infamous owner of no less than a thousand pairs of shoes. The former Miss Manila added glamour to the Marcos campaign. Beneath her glamorous veneer, however, was an ambitious politician, earning her the title of "steel butterfly." To the bitter end of the Marcos regime, she stood by her husband, attempting to rally support for the ousted dictator.

By her own description, President Corazon Aquino, the second famous Filipina in recent times, was a politically inexperienced housewife until the assassination of her husband in 1983 propelled her into the national spotlight. Born in Manila, Corazon Aquino completed her high school and college education in the United States. Her father was a congressman, her mother, a pharmacist. Although she was quiet and reserved, she sought the high-profile and challenging position of president of her troubled country, finding strength in the belief that her cause was just. Integrity and honesty were her hallmarks, qualities that endeared her to a people weary of government fraud and corruption.

When Gloria Macapagal-Arroyo was elected president in 2002, she came to the job well educated and well schooled in the workings of Filipino politics. Macapagal-Arroyo has a Ph.D. in economics and was a classmate of former U.S. president Bill Clinton at Georgetown University in Washington, D.C. She is described as savvy, diplomatic, and intellectual. She is also the daughter of a former president. The January 29, 2001, issue of *Newsweek* magazine introduced her as

a woman accustomed to power—she used to prance through Malacañang [palace] during the presidency of her father, Diosdado Macapagal, in the 1960s—she has prepared herself all her life for this role. Arroyo has obsessively pursued her father's legacy, even reading his memoirs religiously for inspiration and guidance. But she is under no illusions that healing the wounds and rebuilding the economy will be easy.

Gloria Macapagal-Arroyo, one of the Philippines' most influential women, speaks in 2002.

has also fostered stronger relations with the Philippines' Asian neighbors through organizations such as the Association of Southeast Asian Nations. The president has also worked diligently to strengthen ties with the United States, particularly in the fight against global terrorism. However, in 2002, as the future seemed to brighten for Filipinos, Macapagal-Arroyo announced her decision not to run in the 2004 elections, a choice that many found unsettling as well as likely to change. Her statement read in part, "whoever will be elected would still inherit this predicament and the Philippines would be further left behind by its neighbors."[19]

THE STRUGGLING ECONOMY

Despite political upheavals and natural disasters, one aspect of life in the Philippines remains unchanged: It is still a nation of farmers. About 40 percent of the workforce is employed in agriculture, and farm products contributed nearly 20 percent to the gross domestic product in 2001. Equitable distribution of land remains a touchy issue, but the government maintains that the proportion of small farms has been expanding and that nearly 10 million acres of agricultural lands have been distributed to agrarian reform beneficiaries. Under agrarian reform law, a household cannot own a farm larger than 12.4 acres.

Despite efforts at making farming more productive, such as introducing more drought-resistant and high-yield crops, many Filipinos still grow just enough staples to feed their own families. In contrast, foods like sugar, coconut oil, and pineapple, the mainstays of the Philippine export economy, continue to be the domain of larger landholders. Fish, although also a major source of food for Filipino families, is predicted to be one of the country's most lucrative exports in the coming decades. For example, the deep waters off the coast of Mindanao are a plentiful source of tuna, and that industry is growing, although there are disputes with Indonesia over fishing rights. And aquaculture is a fast-growing source of exports, especially to Japan.

The manufacturing sector, which is heavily concentrated in and around Manila, continues to expand. Types of light industry include the manufacture of textiles, pharmaceuticals, chemicals, and wood products. The principal exports, however, are electronics and clothing. In food as well as manufacturing, the Philippine economy continues

Boys harvest sugarcane, the Philippines' most important export. Agriculture remains the foundation of the country's economy.

to depend heavily on the purchasing power of two countries, Japan and the United States.

One significant source of funds for the Philippine economy is not exports or the influx of foreign funds, but rather the money that Filipinos who have gone to foreign lands send back to their families. There are over 2 million Filipinos estimated to be living or working abroad, and they contribute about $7 billion annually to their nation's economy. In Asia, Filipino women often work as maids and nannies. The petroleum refineries of the Middle East have recruited many Filipino men as construction workers. In the United States, many doctors, nurses, and lab technicians are from the Philippines. This trend of working abroad and sending money back home is expected to continue. The downside is that many of the nation's most capable men and women do not put their talents to work for the benefit of their own country. For the most part, these overseas workers are well educated but unable to find suitable jobs at home.

As the Philippine nation enters the twenty-first century, its economy remains closely tied to nature's vagaries, to the robustness of the economy of its major trading partners (the United States and Japan), and to international investors' confidence that the Philippines will ride out its political storms. The United States is the Philippines' largest trading partner, purchasing about one-third of all Philippine exports. It is a two-way street, however, paved with economic benefits for both countries. More than 20 percent of all Philippine imports, valued at over $8 billion, are from the United States.

CATHOLICISM FOR MOST

Just as it remains a nation of farmers, the Philippines remains a nation of Christians. The country's religious makeup has not changed dramatically since the sixteenth century; about 83 percent of the population is Roman Catholic. Although there is an official separation of church and state, the Catholic clergy continue to be criticized for catering to the elite, and they continue to exert a strong influence over politics. The most dramatic examples of their involvement in government affairs were the overthrow of

 ## THE IMPORTANCE OF SUGAR

By the time Ferdinand Magellan arrived in 1521, sugarcane was widely cultivated on the Philippine islands. With the colonization of the archipelago by Spain, sugar became an increasingly important commodity, one that was sought by overseas markets.

Sugar is still an important export, and the principal sugarcane-growing region remains the western Visayas, especially Negros. The tradition of a sugar planter elite continued well into the twentieth century. In *The Philippines: A Country Study*, economist Charles Lindsey traces the history of this phenomenon:

> From the mid-nineteenth century to the mid-1970s, sugar was the most important agricultural export of the Philippines, not only because of the foreign exchange earned, but also because sugar was the basis for the accumulation of wealth of a significant segment of the Filipino elite. The contrast between the sumptuous lifestyles of Negros *hacenderos* and the poverty of their workers, particularly migrant laborers known as *sacadas*, epitomized the vast social and economic gulf separating the elite in the Philippines from the great mass of the population.

Later, free trade agreements with the United States, established in 1913 with its newly acquired colony, protected the Philippines to some extent from fluctuations in the price of sugar on the world market. The United States established quota systems with the Philippines from 1934 through 1974, but even these allowed the Philippines to supply the United States with greater amounts of sugar than suppliers such as Mexico and the Dominican Republic. The world sugar industry continued to be volatile, and prices rose and fell capriciously from the 1970s through the 1990s, partly due to a rise in popularity of sugar substitutes.

two recent presidents, Ferdinand Marcos and Joseph Estrada. About 9 percent of Filipinos are Protestants, mainly as a result of the efforts of American missionaries who arrived in the Philippines after it became an American possession. There are also two indigenous Christian churches: the Iglesia Filipina Independiente (Independent Philippine Church), founded in 1902, which became popular as a result of antifriar, pro-nationalist sentiments; and the Iglesia ni Kristo, or Church of Christ, whose converts were initially recruited among the poorest members of Philippine society.

Despite the apparent uniformity of a mainly Christian society, religious life in the Philippines is complex. The Muslims of the Mindanao and the Sulu Archipelago make up only about 5 percent of the population, but they are a vocal group intent on forming their own state in the southern islands. Indigenous tribes scattered throughout the islands are primarily animists, but they often practice a unique blend of nature worship and Catholic beliefs and rituals. Unlike the situation in neighboring Asian countries, only about 3 percent of the population is Buddhist.

EDUCATION FOR ALL

Whereas the Spanish gave the Philippines Catholicism, the Americans gave the Philippines public schools. As the result of a system introduced after the American occupation, education in the Philippines is free and compulsory. Parents enroll their children, beginning at age seven, for six years of elementary and four years of high school.

Establishing a modern public school system in the Philippines was due in large part to a group of American teachers dubbed the Thomasites. In 1901, this group of dedicated volunteers set out in a converted cattle ship called the *Thomas* to establish a modern public school system throughout the archipelago. They faced natural disasters, tropical diseases, and primitive conditions, but they accomplished their mission.

The system spread by the Thomasites more than a century ago remains intact today, although there have been some changes. Pilipino is now the official language of the public school system. In the 1970s, English was still the language of instruction for students in grades three and up. Today, English is strongly encouraged as a second language, especially for those who aspire to positions in the government or a college education. There are some differences from the U.S. system. Classes

start in June and end in March—when the weather is cool and when seasonal weather events, such as typhoons, are less likely to disrupt classes. Another important difference is that in the Philippines, the national government, rather than local communities, is responsible for providing basic education.

The free-education-for-all policy has resulted in an impressive literacy rate—94 percent—the third highest in Asia. However, not every family has a school nearby or easy transportation to one farther away. Many poor workers cannot afford to spare their children's contribution to the family income. Generally, young people in rural areas have far fewer opportunities to attend school than those in Manila, and so literacy rates are significantly lower. For example, in parts of Mindanao the literacy rate in the early 1990s was 65 percent compared with 95 percent for metropolitan Manila, commonly referred to as Metro Manila.

Although most children attend the free public schools, there are some private elementary and secondary schools, most of them run by religious organizations. Religious groups also oversee many of the nation's 162 colleges and universities. The best known is the University of Santo Tomas, founded by the

Villagers participate in a Palm Sunday procession. Most Filipinos practice some form of Christianity.

Dominican friars in 1611. It is the oldest university in Asia, and in fact its founding predates that of Harvard, the oldest university in the United States.

At the center of the secular higher education system is the University of the Philippines. Established in 1908 by an act of the first Philippine legislature, it is part of the growing University of the Philippines system. From an initial enrollment of fifty in 1909 at the Manila campus, the total count of students had risen to nearly thirty-seven thousand by 1995. University of the Philippines Mindanao is the sixth and newest addition to the system. Besides promoting academic excellence in this heavily Muslim part of the republic, its mission is to promote "social responsibility and nationalism."

FILIPINO FAMILIES IN THE NEW MILLENNIUM

Exposure to American-style education and American culture has brought many changes to Filipino family life.

The infusion of American-style education and American ways of life has brought about significant changes in family life in the Philippines. While the changes are subtle and slow to take hold in agricultural communities, they can be easily

seen in the small but growing middle-class population of urban and suburban dwellers. There are now more educated women and, more importantly, slowly increasing opportunities for them in the urban workforce. Their commitments of time and energy expended to advance in their careers have precipitated changes in the role of men. In families where both partners work outside the home, men are now more involved in caring for children, a role that has traditionally fallen to women.

A sense of community (*bayanihan*) is at the core of Filipino culture, and *bayanihan* begins at home. Strong belief in the family and in children as a blessing that adds true meaning to life is reflected in the country's birthrate, which is one of the highest in the world. However, increasing numbers of young couples are limiting the size of their families, partly due to greater job pressures and the increasing costs of raising a family in a modern society. Most significantly, however, contraceptives are more readily available than they have been in the past, and the Catholic Church's condemnation of birth control seems to be increasingly questioned, at least in urban areas.

Since Spanish colonial times, women have endured a double standard of sexual behavior and have often been treated in a paternalistic manner. The well-known Filipino concept of *amor propio*, translated as protection of dignity or self-esteem, seems to have been applied primarily to men. There is far less acceptance of dysfunctional marriages than in the past, however, and annulments as a way to circumvent the government's refusal to recognize divorce as a legal option are growing in popularity.

The revered Filipino value of *pakikisama*, or social harmony, is likely to be subject to new interpretations in an increasingly industrialized society. *Pakikisama* is based on the premise that if interpersonal relationships are to flourish, individual needs must be secondary to the needs of a partnership or group. Employment and economic pressures, long commutes, less time with family, and raised consciousness concerning the role and rights of women may put this value to the test.

URBAN AND RURAL LIFE

It is in Manila that both the advantages and the challenges of modern life come clearly into focus. What was true at its founding remains true today: Manila is the heart and soul of the country's cultural, political, and economic life. Although Cebu City and Davao in the Visayas and Zamboanga on Mindanao are important as trade centers, Manila is the dominant city and a hub of business and finance. It is also the country's political and judicial capital, a thriving center of arts and entertainment, and home to millions of Filipinos.

Metro Manila is actually a sprawling conglomeration of four cities with a combined population of 12 million people. A small but growing middle class of professionals, civil servants, and businesspeople, not only work in Manila but commute to Metro Manila's many neighborhoods.

In the Makati business district, where many white-collar workers are employed, steel and glass high-rise office buildings, international hotels, and banks reflect the thoroughly modern makeup of the metropolis's most sophisticated area. Manila is not just a magnet for business; it is also a shopping magnet for the country's young, affluent consumers. In many areas, outdoor markets have been replaced by glitzy Western-style malls, which have become phenomenally popular in the Philippines. For scholars, a concentration of fine universities is the draw; for the general population, it is the greater access to television, newspapers, and the Internet. In the midst of this thoroughly modern mix stands the old walled city, the Intramuros, a testimony to a long-ago, but not forgotten, way of life as a Spanish colony.

Manila is not just a contrast of old and new. It is also a contrast of the well-off and the impoverished. Although employed urban dwellers enjoy a much higher standard of living and greater access to social services such as health care and education than those who live in rural areas, there is still a large concentration of desperately poor people in Manila and other urban areas. "Slightly over one half of all urban residents earn below the average income, which is barely enough to keep a family together,"[20] notes Paul Rodell, a specialist in Philippine history and society. Chester Hunt, an author of *The Philippines: A Country Study*, also writes of the abject poverty present in the nation's cities, most notably Manila:

Urban squatters have been a perennial problem or, perhaps, a sign of a problem. Large numbers of people living in makeshift housing, often without water or sewage, indicated that cities had grown in population faster than in

the facilities required. In fact, the growth in population even exceeded the demand for labor so that many squatters found their living by salvaging material from garbage dumps, peddling, and performing irregular day work. Most squatters were long-time residents, who found in the absence of rent a way of coping with economic problems.[21]

Poverty is the norm for more than half of the Philippines' urban population. This family makes their home in a city dump.

While daily life in mainstream Manila focuses on business, daily life in rural areas focuses on survival. Subsistence farming continues to be the main employment in rural areas, with fishing as a strong second source of food and income. Many Filipinos live in *barangays,* or villages, made up a number of *sitios,* or neighborhoods. Often a *barangay* contains a Catholic church and an elementary school but little else. Health care in rural areas is likely to be a combination of modern and traditional medicine. The latter assumes that illness is caused by an action that offends supernatural forces and can be remedied by appeasing them. Educational opportunities and access to mass media have increased, but life in rural areas continues to reflect traditional values that discourage change. The government's efforts to introduce scientific methods that yield fast-growing and more disease-resistant crops have been somewhat successful. Still, many farmers believe that the best way to ensure a good harvest is to perform ancient rituals and honor ancient gods.

The nation's ethnic minorities living in areas such as Luzon's Cordillera Central or the far reaches of the Sulu Archipelago tend to be the Philippine society's most marginalized peoples. Because they make up a small percentage of the population, live in remote areas, are fiercely protective of their land and way of life, and have religious beliefs that are not those of the majority, they remain on the sidelines when it comes to receiving government assistance. Furthermore, government attempts to answer Muslim demands in the southernmost islands have met with limited success, leaving that minority one of the most contentious.

Slowly, and it is hoped surely, the Philippine economy is expanding, bringing the possibility of more employment opportunities and less poverty. Despite living on separate islands and in different cultural climates, the number of Filipinos assimilated into the mainstream society is increasing. More people own land, have access to education and health care, and have their interests represented in government. Filipinos of diverse backgrounds and socioeconomic status are making their voices heard. What they ask for next remains to be seen.

A Vibrant Culture

Spanish, Asian, and American influences plus the traditions of a plethora of indigenous peoples are woven into the Philippine cultural fabric, making it one of the most colorful in the world. Threads of this vibrant culture are evident everywhere—in the events Filipinos celebrate; in their music, dance, and theater performances; in the art and literature that document their experiences; in the food they eat; and in the buildings in which they live, work, and worship. The Filipinos are a people who have been separated by high seas and mountains, assaulted by nature, and imposed upon by foreign powers. With typical Filipino finesse, they have turned hardships into unique blends of artistry.

CELEBRATIONS

Although Filipinos observe a number of secular holidays such as Independence Day (June 12), most national holidays have religious roots that are closely tied to Catholicism but with a uniquely Filipino twist. Holy Week, the week preceding Easter Sunday, is observed with particular fervor. To attract converts, the Spanish introduced the passion play, a reenactment of the suffering of Christ in the days leading up to his death, and Filipinos wholeheartedly embraced the theatricality of the event. During Holy Week, many participate in dramatic and gruesome rites of atonement in various performances throughout the islands.

One example of a communal event based on the sufferings of Christ is the festival of the *Morion* (mask) on the tiny island of Marinduque. The festival reflects the legend of a Roman centurion named Longinus whose sight was returned to his left eye after a drop of Christ's blood touched it. The men of Marinduque create large, colorful wooden or papier-mâché masks symbolizing the face of Longinus and compete for the honor of playing his part in hugely popular reenactments of

Most Filipino holidays and celebrations are religious in nature. Here, a man participates in a festival honoring Jesus.

his conversion to Christianity and subsequent death at the hands of his fellow Romans.

More cheery than Holy Week celebrations, Christmas celebrations are similar to those elsewhere in Christendom, except that Filipinos proudly claim that their Christmastide is the longest in the world. It begins nine days before Christmas with early morning masses and continues until January 6. Parades, fireworks, and decorating towns and homes with star-shaped paper and bamboo lanterns are part of the festivities.

Filipinos also have many local religious celebrations. Each village has a fiesta once a year to honor a Catholic saint. The phenomenon is due largely to the marketing savvy of the Spaniards, who realized the value of celebrations in promoting the spread of Christianity. The Christian tradition of saint worship became entwined with local animist beliefs such as the need to appease local gods in charge of the harvest. As a result, the person named as town saint is often, like the gods, credited with protecting against failed crops. But the saint can also protect against a more localized danger. For example, Santa Ana Kahimonan Abayan, whose festival is held in July on Mindanao, guards against attacks of flesh-eating crocodiles.

A fiesta is held somewhere in the Philippines nearly every month, but May is an especially popular time because it precedes the busiest planting season for many farmers. One of the best known May fiestas is called *pahiya* (precious offerings), named for the agricultural bounty, such as peppers and coconut husks, that people use to decorate the outside of their houses during the event. The most prevalent and elaborately crafted decoration is *kiping*, a rice paste that is dyed an assortment of bright colors, then shaped into large leaves and hardened. *Pahiya* is a tribute to San Isidro Labrador, who was a hardworking farmer from a town near Madrid before being named a saint. The holiday is a time to pray for the saint's blessings as the summer monsoon season begins, but it is also a time to honor the water buffalo, a beast of burden that many Philippine farmers still use to plow their fields.

Another eagerly anticipated event is Ati Atihan, which is celebrated on the island of Panay. This quintessential Filipino fiesta celebrates the Santo Niño, or Christ Child, and commemorates the arrival of a group of Muslim *datus*, or

 ## HANDICRAFTS

Filipinos are an artistic people with a wealth of natural materials at their fingertips, and they make good use of these resources both to enhance their own lives and to boost local economies. Open-air bazaars and upscale malls are filled with a mind-boggling array of native handicrafts of shell, wood, vines, plant fibers, and metals. Just about every region in the country has specialties, based on available materials, cultural practices, and religious beliefs.

Enterprising Filipinos on Panay turn readily available capiz shells into fashionable jewelry, lampshades, chimes, even chandeliers. Forests and beaches are a source of craft materials. Originally used to store grain or catch fish, baskets of all shapes and sizes are popular items to produce and sell because rattan grows so abundantly in rain forests. Baskets from different parts of the Philippines can be distinguished by their designs, colors, and the materials from which they are crafted.

The T'boli people in southwest Mindanao also make use of forest materials for one of their most sought-after specialties, *t'nalak* cloth, which is woven from strands of abaca fiber that are extracted from the plant by hand. *T'nalak* clothing complements the T'boli's beautifully crafted brass jewelry, but they also turn *t'nalak* cloth into such items as placemats and scarves for shoppers in Manila. Filipinos also capitalize on the abundant grasses and even fruits growing in the countryside to fashion clothing. Ramie, a popular fabric similar to linen, is woven from grass fibers. *Piña*, a delicate material woven from pineapple fibers, is used to make clothing that is then embroidered with intricate designs.

leaders, migrating from Borneo in the thirteenth century. Legend has it that the incoming *datus* made friends with the dark-skinned natives, the Atis. Then, to celebrate the peace pact, the *datus* painted their faces with soot to make themselves look more like their animist hosts. The tradition lives on today, with Filipinos painting their faces and participating in Mardi Gras–style merrymaking—singing, dancing, banging on gongs and cymbals, dressing in elaborate costumes, and joining in holy processions to honor Santo Niño.

Fiestas are not just religious occasions—they are community events that strengthen social bonds and local pride: Towns often compete for "best" fiesta. Fiestas typically include such worldly activities as beauty contests, sporting events, family reunions, speeches, cockfights, and, of course, feasting on local foods.

MUSIC

In a country so fond of celebrating, music plays a major role in the entertainment. The Spaniards introduced songs intended to instruct in religious principles and to enliven stories of the saints. Later, the Americans introduced an array of Western music such as ragtime, jazz, rock and roll, and rap. Despite the influx of foreign styles, many ethnic traditions that predate Spanish and American invasions have survived—some because they are preserved in remote locations, other because they have been adapted to appeal to nationalist sentiments.

One of the most enduring of the indigenous musical forms is the *kundiman*, which originated with the Tagalog people. Intended as a love song, the *kundiman* usually involves the brokenhearted pleadings of a male suitor, but it can also carry a political message. A patriotic poem called "Bayan Ko" (My Country) became a *kundiman* when set to music in 1928. It endured as the anthem of nationalists during the Marcos martial law period and was sung in 1986 by hundreds of thousands of Manila's citizens participating in the People Power Revolution. The sentimental ballad style of the *kundiman* continues to inspire today. One of the most enduring hits of popular singer Freddy Aguilar is "Anak" (Child), in which he combines Western music with a distinctly Filipino-style song that praises family values.

Whether they live in the Cordillera Central of northern Luzon, the remotest parts of the Visayan Islands, or the far reaches of the Sulu Archipelago, Filipinos seem to have a song for every occasion, from birth to blessing a marriage to burying the dead. The Tingyans in northern Luzon express friendship and love in the *salagintok*. Rural Filipinos have work songs to pass the time while hunting, fishing, carrying water, weaving, and harvesting rice. The Bontok can be heard singing their most famous work song, the *annoay*, while maintaining their rice terraces. Filipinos also preserve the epic stories of their culture through songs. For example, the Tausugs have the "Luguh Maulud," a song that celebrates the birth of the Prophet Muhammad.

Traditional instruments that frequently accompany singing are typically made of bamboo, brass, and wood. The *git-git*, however, is a fiddlelike instrument sometimes made with abaca fibers and sometimes with human hair. Other stringed instruments frequently heard are the zither and the

Men sing and bang wooden staffs to keep the rhythm during a festival celebration. Music is an important part of Filipino culture.

kutyapi, a two-string lute played in Mindanao. The bamboo flute is common throughout the islands, although its shape and size varies with locale. When it is time to make music, Filipinos will use just about anything at hand, from sticks to shells. The most memorable indigenous instrument, however, remains the gong, which can be struck rhythmically to accompany singing and dancing. Brass gongs of all sorts—some handheld, some suspended on wooden frames, some arranged by increasing size and played like a xylophone—are capturing the attention of modern musicians, who are including them in their newest compositions.

DANCE

Many musicians now favor complex blends of imported and indigenous styles, but in dance genres, there continue to be clear-cut lines between old and new. The latest Western dances, usually those in vogue in America, are the most popular in urban centers like Manila. But rich rural traditions stemming from a Malay, Muslim, and Spanish heritage are also very much alive in the Philippines and have remained relatively unchanged over time.

A traditional Malay dance often performed in the Philippines is the *tinikling*. In it, a dancer mimics the agile movements of the *tinikling* bird. The dancer must step quickly

Muslim dancers in traditional dress prepare for a performance of the singkil, *a dance involving elegant costumes and brightly colored handkerchiefs.*

between bamboo poles that are beaten against each other to simulate traps set by farmers to capture the *tinikling* as it moves through the rice fields. Bamboo poles are also a part of the *singkil*, a rousing Muslim dance with numerous variations, many of them improvised. In Maranao legend, the *singkil* is the dance of a light-footed princess who skips over falling trees and rocks during an earthquake caused by a mischievous wood nymph. Predictably, the cast of characters also includes a prince. Performers wearing elegant costumes and usually waving enormous fans or brightly colored handkerchiefs weave expertly through bamboo poles that in this case are rhythmically clapped together to represent the fallen trees.

While many folk dances express the rituals of courtship, war also plays an important role in Filipino dances. For mountain peoples in the north and Muslims in the south, dances prepare young men for battle, and the victories of returning heroes are dramatized in celebratory dances. For those who do not return, a dance, accompanied by bells and other loud music, calls their spirits home so they will not be destined to wander the earth.

It was not until the more relaxed atmosphere of the nineteenth century that dances from Spain made their way into Philippine life. These, of course, were modified to suit local tastes. For example, the fandango, a lively Iberian folk dance, evolved into the *pandanggo*. There are many versions of the *pandanggo*. One of the most popular features a female dancer balancing oil lamps on the backs of her hands and on her head while performing a series of intricate crossover steps.

THEATER

Theatrical traditions in the Philippines can be traced to two genres that reflect age-old conflicts. The first is called the *moro-moro*, a play written in verse that portrays conflicts between early Christians and Muslims. Predictably, the Spanish colonists used the *moro-moro* as a way to spread their religious message. After Philippine theaters were constructed in the nineteenth century, Filipinos countered with the zarzuela, a satirical form of opera that they adapted to criticize colonial ploys and policies.

In modern times, a well-respected author is National Artist for Literature Nick Joaquin. National Artist Awards are

JEEPNEYS

Jeepneys, the colorful minibuses seen everywhere in the Philippines, evolved from jeeps left behind by American troops after World War II. At first, Filipinos extended the frame of the jeep so that two rows of facing seats (holding up to seventeen people) could be installed in the back. The name *jeepney* was coined by combining *jeep* and *jitney* (a small bus). The jeepney almost defies description, but can be best viewed as a mobile form of pop art.

Unlike bus drivers in the United States, jeepney drivers are free to individualize their vehicles, and as a result, all are unique visual treats. On the outside, jeepneys are painted vibrant colors and adorned with additional lights, mirrors, antennae streamers, and fancy hood decorations. Local companies and politicians may post advertisements, and the proud owners often emblazon their nicknames on the front. Almost as an afterthought, the route the jeepney will take, at least in theory, will appear on a sign above the windshield, although it may be difficult to pick out amid the other religious and inspirational slogans.

On the inside, the creativity continues. A shrine with garlands of sweet-smelling *sampaguita* flowers and statues of St. Christopher, the patron saint of travelers, or the Virgin Mary is among the first objects to greet passengers boarding the jeepney. Other items may include a fan to reduce the oppressive heat, photos of family members or movie stars, personal memorabilia, tapes and a cassette player for everyone's listening enjoyment, and a box for depositing fares. Even the ceiling and the curtains hung along the open sides of the passenger area may be decorated.

When the supply of World War II surplus jeeps ran out, Filipinos began to manufacture their beloved jeepneys from scratch. The newer stainless steel version of the jeepney is more suited to the seaside environment—and traffic conditions—of the Philippines. Its stainless steel body will not rust or dent easily, and its seats are padded with coconut husks.

Colorfully decorated minibuses known as jeepneys are a common form of art and transportation.

the highest honors given to Filipino artists. Nick Joaquin's best-known full-length play is aptly titled *Portrait of the Artist as Filipino*. Written in English, this drama is set right before World War II and deals with Western influences on Filipino identity. Western theater continues to be well received in the Philippines, and Filipino tastes generally lean toward productions that feature much music and dance. *Miss Saigon* remains a perennial favorite because Filipina Lea Salonga achieved international fame for her lead role as Kim in the long-running Broadway production.

Painting

Although many people associate Philippine creative expression with the performing arts, a number of world-renowned Filipinos are painters. In the nineteenth century, Juan Luna depicted epic scenes, often with an eye to giving them social significance. His most famous work, *Spolarium*, features fallen Roman gladiators but is said to be a subtle criticism of Spain's colonial rule. It is interesting that Luna, who was heavily influenced by Spanish trends in art, achieved international fame and a gold medal at the 1894 Madrid Exposition, Spain's most prestigious art competition, while managing to use his talents to disparage colonial policies.

Twentieth century painter Fernando Amorsolo was the Philippines' first National Artist for the Visual Arts. He is best known for rustic scenes such as *Resting by the Ricefield* and for renditions of historic events such as Magellan's landing on Cebu and the first baptism performed on the island. Amorsolo's idealized portrayals of life were challenged by post–World War II artists who leaned toward cubism and abstraction and who wanted to portray the negative as well as the positive side of Filipinos' experiences. Vicente Manansala is one of the best known of modern Filipino artists interested in social realism. Manansala's most compelling work, titled *Madonna of the Slums*, is a stark portrait of a destitute mother and child.

Present-day artists such as Arlene Villaver continue the tradition of portraying ordinary people struggling against the sometimes harsh realities of life in the Philippines. She has commented,

> I often paint victims of calamities such as the Aetas [an indigenous tribe in central Luzon] in the 1990 earthquake

and the Mount Pinatubo eruption. I try to depict their sense of struggle as well as the hope they continue to feel. I work on the facial expressions by trying to internalize them. Sometimes I look at my face in the mirror and ask: How would I feel if, like them, I were sad, lost, and in pain? What would my eyes look like?[22]

LITERATURE

Compared to other art forms, Filipino literature was relatively free from colonial influences, at least for the first three hundred years of Spanish occupation. This was mainly because the Spaniards did not want to teach their language, and thus its literature, to the natives. For a long time, the only printed materials distributed by the Spanish were such items as prayer books, hymnals, catechisms, and the story of the death of Christ—materials that could be used for religious instruction. The friars then translated these books into various local dialects and distributed them. Because Filipinos were not exposed to European literature, they were able to preserve their own stories that had been passed on from generation to generation without having been written down. Many of these were no more than riddles or proverbs loosely woven into stories of everyday life and love to entertain friends and family while sitting around a fire at night or working in the fields. Some, like the Tagalog folktale "Juan Tamad," are about the adventures of an imaginary character. Others are fables, such as "The Tortoise and the Monkey," popularized by Filipino revolutionary writer José Rizal. Most complex and lasting of the oral traditions, however, are the epic stories that tell of the amazing deeds of heroes and gods. Crafted by skilled storytellers, they often contain the core beliefs and values of a society. Famous epics include *Hudhud and Alim* from the Ifugao tribe and *Biag ni Lam-ang* (The Life of Lam-ang) from the Ilocano tribe.

Once Spanish was available to educated Filipinos, it, not any of the country's many dialects, became the national language. Ironically, through Spanish, Filipinos were able to transcend regional linguistic differences and promote a national consciousness that would lead to the fall of the colonial power. It was in Spanish, after all, that José Rizal published his accounts of the harshness of Spanish rule in *Noli Me Tangere* and *El Filibusterismo*.

The emphasis on American education after the United States took over the role of colonial overseer in the Philippines eventually resulted in a number of Filipino writers creating works in English. Despite the constraints of expressing ideas in a foreign language, José Garcia Villa wrote a number of widely acclaimed poems in English. Nick Joaquin also writes in English. During the troubled Marcos years, the continuing search for a national identity inspired many writers to choose Tagalog as a medium for expression while continuing to utilize English. Historian Paul Rodell writes,

> Although precise dating is difficult, the contemporary period of Philippine literature can be said to have begun in the 1960s during the rule of President Ferdinand Marcos. In keeping with its oral and poetic origins, poets who wrote in Tagalog, but who are equally versatile in English initiated the contemporary period. Additionally, some younger writers began to experiment with Taglish, a hip urban mixing of English and Tagalog that gives the writer additional linguistic complexity to craft double meanings and situations of social satire.[23]

Whether they write in Tagalog, English, or a unique combination of both, the nation's writers have not forgotten the oppression of the past or the plight of the poor. In novels and poems, powerful critiques of Philippine society continue to be popular.

Cuisine

Like other aspects of culture, the cuisine of the Philippines is a showcase for the nation's checkered past and present. Filipinos have adapted the recipes of many nations, using available ingredients and appealing to local tastes. The differences from locale to locale are mainly in the sauces, which can be sweet, sour, or spicy. Because coconut is so abundant, it is a major ingredient in many dishes, giving foods that were originally introduced by foreigners a distinctly Filipino flavor. The Spaniards' main dish, paella, is a good example. In the Philippines, paella became *bringhe* and is flavored with coconut milk instead of olive oil and saffron. *Adobo*, a vegetable and meat stew, is similar to a Spanish dish called *adobado*. *Adobo* has many regional variations, depending on the local vegetables and poultry or livestock

TROPICAL FRUITS

As a result of the warm climate and abundant rainfall, a dazzling array of tropical fruits flourishes in the Philippines. Bananas are probably the most readily available fruit in the country because they are so easy to cultivate. Shoppers have as many as fifty varieties from which to pick. Among the most popular are *latundan,* described as oblong with whitish flesh; *lacatan,* long and slender with yellowish flesh; and *senoritas,* little ones perfect for snacking. The largest, the *baston,* is a popular export. Bananas find their way into all kinds of desserts and even into a Spanish-inspired main dish, tamales, which Filipinos wrap in banana leaves rather than corn husks.

Pineapples, papayas, and avocados, which were originally brought by Spanish galleons sailing from Mexico, still grow well. Filipinos prefer their ripe papayas chilled with a squeeze of lime or made into preserves, jams, and juices. Coconut is the most versatile fruit on the islands. Coconut meat is cut into pieces and eaten raw or grated and added to main dishes and desserts. Meats and fish are often cooked in coconut milk, and a fermented drink called *tuba* is made from coconut.

Fruits less familiar to Westerners are the durian, which has a distinctly pungent taste, and milder, sweeter fruits such as the mangosteen and *lanzone.* The *langka* (jackfruit) is one of the largest fruits in the world, growing to two feet long, and is covered with short spines. A ripe *langka* has a distinct aroma that attracts birds and insects, so Filipinos often wrap it in plastic even while it is still growing. *Langka* preserves are often used in *halo-halo* (mix-mix), an icy and colorful concoction of local fruits, coconut, beans, and gelatin.

Although most fruits found in the Philippines can be eaten as is, some are used mainly as souring agents in cooking. *Sinigang,* a versatile local entrée that may include any meat or fish and just about any vegetables, derives its signature flavor from the addition of one or more acidic fruits such as lime, guava, tamarind, or green mango. The sour broth is said to have a cooling effect that is a welcome sensation in a tropical climate.

available, but it is typically cooked with vinegar, garlic, soy sauce, and chili peppers.

Chinese dishes, particularly noodles, became popular almost as soon as they were introduced into the Philippines by Chinese merchants long ago. The merchants were of a similar socioeconomic class as the Filipinos, and the climate they came from was also similar. Unlike the ingredients found in many of the dishes introduced by the Spanish elite, the merchants' staples could be easily grown or an acceptable substitute could be easily found.

The American contribution to Filipino cuisine initially focused on more sanitary food preparation techniques for the Filipino cooks and more "sophisticated" recipes for them to try, namely those that reflected American tastes. The trend later expanded to technological advances such as gas and electric stoves versus coal- and wood-burning ones. The hallmark of American cuisine is now convenience, and fast-food restaurants offering such choices as hamburgers are popular with busy families in urban areas. However, Filipinos claim to have had their own versions of fast foods long before the U.S. influx. Street vendors and sidewalk stands sell a variety of tempting treats. *Turo-turo* (point-point) is the time-honored way for customers to sample a food vendor's wares by peering into an assortment of containers and pointing to the dishes they prefer.

Filipino cuisine reflects the country's history, but it also reflects its geography. The Philippines' tropical location equates to warm temperatures and abundant rainfall, resulting in a nearly continuous growing season for its main staple, rice. As in many countries in Asia, rice is at the center of the culture as well as the basic source of sustenance in the Philippines. It is a part of every meal, including breakfast, and it is featured in just about every delicacy. The "proper" way to cook rice is one of the first things children learn. The importance of rice is also reflected in the language. For example, the word for cooked rice, *kanin,* is the root word for the Pilipino verbs meaning "to eat" and "to feed people." Rice is supplemented with locally grown vegetables and with meat or fish, the latter always available in this island nation.

Because they live in a warm environment where meat and fish easily go bad, Filipinos created *kinelaw.* In this age-old process, which is also the name of the dish itself, fish or meats such as goat are marinated in lime juice and vinegar. The acids in these two liquids "cook" the raw foods without the use of heat, thus preventing spoilage. An archaeological site on Mindanao contains remnants of a *kinelaw* that is at least a thousand years old. Roasting is another popular way to prepare meats, and *lechon* (suckling pig) can be found everywhere from banquet tables to street stalls. *Lechon* is cooked over an open fire, stuffed with various spices, and served with sauces that vary with the locale but are often made with liver.

ARCHITECTURE

Like its flavorful dishes, the architecture of the Philippines tells much about the country's past and its physical environment. Foreign-built edifices, native structures built to withstand the ravages of nature, and blends of both styles create a skyline—in the countryside and in the city—that is unmistakably Filipino.

One of the country's most impressive structures, and one that is certainly linked to its past, is the Intramuros, the thick-walled city that was the original Manila. Built to protect against seafaring invaders, it resembled a European medieval town with moats and drawbridges. The sheltered space inside its massive walls was reserved for government buildings, churches, and residences of church officials and other members of the elite. Although the site was bombed during World War II, a few historic buildings remain inside the Intramuros, most notably San Agustin Church and the ruins of Fort Santiago. Built in 1587 by Filipino and Chinese artisans, San Agustin is an excellent example of the ornate baroque style so popular with the Spanish conquerors.

Once firmly entrenched in Manila, the Spaniards spent three and a half centuries fortifying the coastline with places for their new converts to worship. The friars in charge of such construction thought that churches built from lowly materi-

Many suburban Filipino homes incorporate indigenous architectural elements like the steep roof of this traditional hut.

als such as bamboo and grass would not be fitting places for Christian communities to gather. So they commissioned finer churches, often with thick walls embellished with local materials such as coral, limestone, and even sugar. These churches were built to pay tribute to a powerful God and to withstand natural disasters. Filipino historians coined the term "earthquake baroque" for these structures.

Around 1904, American architect William Parsons introduced a neoclassical design for the Philippines' new government buildings so their style would mirror that of government buildings in the United States. The columned style took hold both in the capital and in the provinces. Parsons also created fifteen basic floor plans for another American construction priority, schoolhouses.

Although Manila contains a mixture of Spanish-era churches, American-era government buildings, and contemporary structures of steel and glass, Filipino architects are introducing indigenous materials and styles into the eclectic mix. The headquarters of the San Miguel Corporation, designed by Manuel, Jose, and Francisco Manosa, is a modern building with tiered balconies intended to represent the famous rice terraces of the Cordillerra Central. Gabriel Formoso designed the Asian Institute of Management building in the style of the *bahay na bato*, or house of stone, with stone walls and wooden panels. Leandro Locsin, who designed the Cultural Center of the Philippines with concrete walls for the center's main theater made widespread use of native designs and materials. Focal points of the Cultural Center are the capiz shell chandeliers in the lobby. It is not just the high-rise canyons of business districts like Makita that sport indigenous touches. Although older suburbs were modeled on American style suburban homes, newer residences combine traditional architectural elements, such as the steep roof and protective eaves of the *bahay kubo*, or native hut, with contemporary lines and the newest construction materials.

With great artistry, Filipinos have embraced all the experiences that nature and history have bestowed on them and created a culture that is rich and diverse. It is a heritage of a people who seek a bright future but who are determined not to leave the treasure of the past behind.

6

THE SEARCH
FOR STABILITY

The Philippines is a nation of resilient people who are blessed with rich resources and a beautiful land. However, the possibility of a bright future is clouded by several interrelated problems. The major obstacle to this nation's future success, and one that is tied to all its other problems, is poverty. Despite the country's high literacy rate and public education system, only 20 percent of the people are classified as middle-class. In the year 2000, the poor constituted 40 percent of the population, and some critics believe they are getting poorer. Unfortunately, the Philippines is a nation in which there is a huge disparity between the haves and have-nots, and the wealthy have little incentive to help the poor. When President Macapagal-Arroyo took office, she pledged to eradicate poverty within ten years. While most people agree that this is a noble goal, many experts see it as an unrealistic one. Efforts to achieve economic stability, and thereby eliminate poverty, are closely connected to the other major problems faced by the Philippines: the unpredictability of nature, environmental degradation, a burgeoning population, terrorism, and a continuing crisis of confidence.

ON THE BRINK OF DISASTERS
One of the country's major problems, the unpredictability of nature, has, at least for now, few comprehensive solutions. The Philippines has the dubious distinction of being one of the most disaster-prone places on earth. Typhoons and monsoons often bring floods. El Niño events originating in Pacific waters have been blamed for devastating droughts in recent years. Earthquakes and their underwater counterparts, tsunamis, are frequent. Volcanic eruptions, actual and potential, are a way of life. The 1991 eruption of Mount Pinatubo, the third largest in the twentieth century, is a good example of the ripple effect of

volcanic eruptions. In the rainy seasons of recent years, mud-slides and lahars caused by the eruption still plague farmers trying to plant crops on the volcano's fertile slopes. And scientists are still assessing the eruption's effects on greenhouse warming and the ozone layer. All of these natural phenomena threaten lives and affect employment, the economy, and the environment.

The eruption of Mount Pinatubo led to the closing of the U.S. military bases on the islands. The move caused economic hardship for both Filipinos and Americans and continued ill-will between the two countries. Ten years later, its effect on U.S.-Philippine relations continued to be a topic of concern. Richard Fisher Jr., a senior fellow at the Jamestown Foundation in Washington, D.C., made the case for putting aside hard feelings still harbored from the closing of U.S. military bases. At a U.S. Senate hearing before the Subcommittee on East Asian and Pacific Affairs he said:

I think it is time for us to consider the past and the future of the Philippine-American alliance. This alliance has seen enormous shared sacrifice and, while a military bases relationship ended in 1991 and 1992 that left anger and bitterness on both sides, I think now that a decade has passed there is very encouraging new willingness on

Filipinos displaced by the 1991 eruption of Mount Pinatubo beg for money on the streets of Quezon City.

the part of Manila to reach out and try to build a sustainable long-term military relationship.[24]

DEFORESTATION

Aside from the fallout from volcanic eruptions (ash in the air and on crops and the dangers of lahars), the Philippines faces other serious environmental issues. A significant one is deforestation. Rain forests once stretched across many of the large islands, but these exotic ecosystems are shrinking with alarming speed. The lumber industry and urban development have claimed much of the land, and the deforestation has threatened the existence of many of the nation's rare and endangered plants and animals.

Loggers steer logs toward a Mindanao sawmill. Deforestation caused by logging threatens many of the Philippines' endangered plants and animals.

From an economic viewpoint, there is no question that trees are the most important plant in the Philippines. Some fifty years ago, the country's forests were valued at $20 billion at least. Hungry for a lucrative source of income for the struggling economy, the government made commercial logging a national priority. In *The Philippines: A Country Study*, economist Charles W. Lindsey gives the history of a time when loggers in search of valuable hardwoods were encouraged to denude the land:

> The government facilitated the exploitation of the country's forest resources for the first three decades after independence by allocating the bulk of unclassified land as public forest land eligible to be licensed for logging, and by implementing policies of low forest charges and export taxes. Logs were a major foreign-exchange earner. By 1977, 8.3 million hectares of forest area were licensed for logging. In the late 1970s, the government became aware of the dangers of deforestation and began to impose restrictions.[25]

Although the percentage of logs and lumber in total Philippine exports declined from 25 percent in 1969 to 2 percent in 1988 and there is now a moratorium on logging, the turnabout may be too little too late. In the early 1950s, forests covered more than 53 percent of the islands. By 2003, more than 70 percent of the nation's original forests had been destroyed. Vast stands of hardwood trees do remain on Palawan and Mindanao, but their loss could mean a timber famine in the coming decades.

In addition to the legal logging industry, there has always been considerable illegal logging in the Philippines. A crackdown on such illegal activity continues, but in a country of more than seven thousand islands, enforcing the law is difficult. Because this is a clandestine pursuit, the degree to which it exists is difficult to determine. One way the Philippine government does the math, however, is to look at the discrepancy between its own and Japanese trade records. In the heyday of logging, log imports from the Philippines according to Japanese statistics averaged about 50 percent more than log exports to Japan according to Philippines statistics. The discrepancy is now considerably smaller, indicating that a stricter enforcement policy has been successful.

Another cause of deforestation is swidden, or slash-and-burn, agriculture. Upland Filipino groups have often depended on this traditional method. It entails burning a portion of the forest, planting a series of crops for two or three years, and then, after the soil has become depleted of nutrients, moving to another location. The practice is ecologically sound as long as the burned-out area is allowed enough time to rejuvenate. However, increased use of land for logging and migration of landless peasants from lowland areas have decreased the amount of land available for farming. When soil is not allowed to lie fallow for a sufficient period and when new trees cannot mature before being burned again, extensive erosion occurs, and forests become nutrient-poor grasslands.

MINING

In addition to lumber, the Philippines is rich in mineral resources, but as with lumber, capitalizing on these underground resources comes with an environmental price to pay. The Mining Act of 1995 gave the Philippine government more control of mining operations; it was implemented in an attempt to bolster a sagging economy. The strategy, like so many others in the Philippines, has met with opposition. Among those who voiced their disapproval were the country's influential Catholic bishops. Part of a drafted statement reads:

We want to tell you how concerned we are at the rapid expansion of mining operations arising from the Mining Act of 1995. . . .

Through Agreements arising from the Mining Act our land is being offered to foreign owned companies with liberal conditions, while our people continue to grow in poverty. Through the Financial or Technical Assistance Agreements a significant portion of our country is being offered for large-scale mining operations. Our land is rich, yet over-exploitation threatens the future of our people. We must therefore guard our non-renewable resources, like minerals, to ensure sustainable development of our land for the sake of future generations. We have seen the devastating effects of some of the mining operations: the spillages of mine tailings. . . . The adverse social impact on the affected communities, specially on our indigenous brothers and sisters far outweigh the gains promised by large-scale mining corporations. Our people living in the mountains and along the affected shorelines can no longer avail of the bounty of nature. Rice-fields are devastated and bays rich with sea foods become health hazards. Implementation of the Mining Act will certainly destroy both environment and people and will lead to national unrest.... Hence, we ask for the repeal of Republic Act 7942 known as the Philippine Mining Act of 1995.[26]

The Macapagal administration has amended the Mining Act in attempts to address the concerns voiced by the Catholic bishops, but mining policies continue to be a balancing act between bolstering the economy and protecting the environment.

OCEAN ENVIRONMENT

Delicate balancing acts are also part of the country's efforts to reap the benefits of its vast territorial waters. Along coasts, mangrove trees are the habitat of hundreds of marine species for which they provide food and protection. Ironically, many of these swamps have been cleared to create aquaculture pools, an increasingly important export.

Beyond the land-water borders of the diminishing mangrove swamps, coral reefs have been seriously damaged by fishing with dynamite and cyanide, and by *muro-ami*, a technique in which fishermen pound the coral with rocks attached to ropes to drive fish into their nets. Such irresponsible fishing practices, which threaten the destruction of the coral reef ecosystem, are now illegal, and the country is looking for environmentally sound ways to increase its commercial catch and to provide its impoverished seaside communities with better ways to utilize the waters that surround them.

Fishing is not the only industry having an adverse impact on the ocean environment. Tourism, although it is an industry that the country tries hard to promote, does have a downside. Borocay, an island just off the northeastern tip of Panay, is a case in point. In the 1980s, adventuresome vacationers from America, Europe, and Asia who were looking for an unusual destination "discovered" Borocay. Attracted by its white sands and warm waters, they soon turned the tiny island into a showcase resort. While such an influx of visitors was good for the economy, it was bad for the ecology. Tourists were dumping their sewage into Borocay's once-clear waters, and by 1997, the

THE CONTROVERSIAL SAN ROQUE DAM

The San Roque Dam on the Agno River in the Cordillera Central, if completed, will be the tallest dam and largest private hydropower project in Asia, generating megawatts of power, mainly for Luzon. The dam is also expected to irrigate nearly fifty thousand acres of farmland. The project began in 1998 and is slated for completion in 2004. Although it will supply much-needed energy, the project is fiercely opposed by thousands of indigenous Ibaloi peoples upstream of the dam site. The Cordillera Peoples' Alliance estimates that if the multibillion-dollar dam is built, it will submerge more than twenty thousand hectares of farmland and displace more than thirty-five thousand indigenous people living upstream in the province of Benguet. More than six hundred families have already been evicted.

The government's position is that some sixty thousand families will directly benefit because the project will improve the irrigation system and that the dam will also help prevent the perennial flooding caused by the Agno River, which affects at least sixteen towns and causes losses in the millions of pesos due to lost harvests. President Macapagal-Arroyo wants to arrive at a win-win solution that provides power for the majority population without invoking the ire of indigenous tribes and environmentalists.

Government officials have assured families affected by the project that they will receive adequate compensation for any loss of land or livelihood.

Ibaloi natives protest the building of the San Roque Dam.

Philippine Department of Health declared those waters severely polluted. Bacteria levels are now closely monitored in the seas around Borocay and other destination islands in the Philippines.

OVERPOPULATION

The population of the Philippines is growing, and the growth has contributed to poverty, pollution, rural-to-urban migrations, and an increased drain on city services. Those who migrate to Manila in search of economic opportunities and a so-phisticated lifestyle seldom find them. Instead, they find them-selves jobless and living in crowded, unsanitary, unsafe conditions. Metro Manila, currently supporting a population of more than 11 million, has grown far beyond expectations. For the underprivileged, the quality of life is not much better in smaller cities, a number of which have attained populations of over 1 million.

In a country in which birth control is discouraged, demog-raphers predict that the accelerated pace of population growth is likely to continue and that over half the population will soon live in cities. In fact, rural communities and farmland are giv-ing way to urban development at an alarming rate.

As a result of its growing population, one of the country's most dire needs is increased energy supplies. The need for electricity is increasing at an annual rate of 9 percent. Hydro-electric dams currently supply 20 percent of energy needs, and natural gas production is under way. The lack of reliable power has become a serious bottleneck to the country's con-tinued economic growth, because commercial enterprises, both foreign and domestic, are leery of investing in a nation that cannot guarantee adequate power supplies. President Macapagal-Arroyo has supported legislation to restructure the nation's power industry, in particular the government-owned National Power Corporation, so that private industry can play a greater role.

TERRORISM

The country's valiant efforts to create a stable setting for in-vestment have been tainted by a deadly new concern, terror-ism. As the twenty-first century opened, several highly publicized events led the world to associate the Philippines with terrorism, an association that hardly entices international corporations or tourists. In 2001, the Philippine terrorist group Abu Sayyaf, which some experts say is linked to Osama bin Laden's Middle East terrorist organization, al-Qaeda, kidnapped two American missionaries and a Filipino nurse. In October 2002, bombings in Mindanao's port city of Zamboanga were blamed on that same group. By February 2003, the government was consid-ering sending U.S. troops to join the fight against Abu Sayyaf rebels operating on the islands of Basilan and Jolo. Ensuring se-curity in the impoverished region, however, is likely to depend not on military action but on lessening the appeal of Abu Sayyaf by ad-dressing the basic economic needs of the people.

The 7 million Muslims on Mindanao and in the Sulu Archipelago are among the poorest people in the Philippines, and it is poverty that has fed their long-running conflict with the government. They harbor a long history of grievances against a government run by Christians in far-off Manila and dominated by the interests of Luzon and the central Visayas. Although they live in a region that is rich in natural resources, they are often the last of the nation's citizens to reap the benefits. The southern peoples pay taxes but believe that they have little say in how revenues are spent. Furthermore, they resent the lowland Christian Filipinos' continuous encroachment on their ancestral land.

In the 1970s, Philippine Muslims, citing economic discrimination based on cultural and religious differences between themselves and the country's Christian majority, rallied as the Moro National Liberation Front (MNLF) and initiated demands for an independent state in the south. After years of fighting between MNLF and government forces, an agreement was finally reached in 1996 to create an autonomous Muslim region. However, a splinter group of MNLF, the Moro Islamic Liberation Front (MILF), continues to battle for an independent state governed by Koranic principles. Abu Sayyaf, which

The Moro Islamic Liberation Front wants to establish an independent Islamic government within the Philippines.

supports the goal of complete independence, recruits many of its members from the ranks of MILF—and some observers suspect that MILF recruits many of its members from the ranks of the terrorists.

MILF has built a strong political and military base in the Philippines. Many of its leaders are said to have gained military experience by training with Islamic extremists in Pakistan and fighting with al-Qaeda forces in Afghanistan. Estimates of its armed troops range from 15,000 to 120,000. A frustrating development is that some young men from impoverished families join the Muslim guerrillas not because they support their cause but because they are paid for their service in the militia.

One of President Macapagal-Arroyo's top priorities is to eliminate the economic causes of the country's crippling discontent by accelerating economic development, particularly on Mindanao. One strategy is to allow Mindanao to increase trade with its neighbors in Malaysia and Indonesia, with whom religiously and culturally the Muslims have much more in common than with their fellow Filipinos.

Filipinos have plenty of incentives for seeking a peaceful solution to the violence. The fighting in the south is estimated to cost the country as much as $20 million a month. Such spending leads to larger budget deficits, has a negative impact on economic growth and investors' confidence, and perpetuates the cycle of poverty.

CRISIS OF CONFIDENCE

Although President Macapagal-Arroyo has done much to restore honesty in government, political corruption and crony capitalism, the hallmarks of the Marcos and Estrada administrations, have left a negative imprint on the Philippines that is difficult to erase. In recent years, two revolutions have rocked the Philippines, and in their aftermath, each incoming president has expended considerable energy attempting to regain the trust not only of Filipinos but also of the world community.

Battling uneasiness among allies and investors over the future of the Philippines, President Macapagal-Arroyo has worked hard to regain the support and respect of neighboring countries, especially through the Association of Southeast Asian Nations (ASEAN). There is no scarcity of issues to challenge ASEAN, a ten-country organization whose aims include promoting economic development and peaceful resolution of regional conflicts. In addition to the region being a hotbed of terrorist activity, there have been sporadic attacks on commercial vessels by modern-day pirates and disputes between Indonesians and Filipinos over deep-sea fishing rights. Most recently, as the energy needs of Southeast Asia balloon, there has been a huge controversy over who owns the oil that likely lies beneath the South China Sea near the remote Spratly Islands. Although preliminary investigations indicate that oil lies there, the area remains largely unexplored because China, Taiwan, Vietnam, Malaysia, and the Philippines all claim ownership of at least some of the Spratlys and have interfered, sometimes violently, with one another's efforts at oil recovery.

In 1995, the Philippines discovered four buildings on an out-of-the-way atoll in the South China Sea that is appropriately named Mischief Reef. The buildings had been erected by the People's Republic of China. The reef is about 150 miles away from Palawan, at the east end of the Spratly Islands. Most significantly, the islands fall well within the Philippines' internationally recognized two-hundred-mile exclusive economic zone, which is the sea surrounding a country that can be claimed as its territory for fishing and exploiting other natural resources that lie beneath the sea. Furthermore, the Spratlys lie over eight hundred miles away from the Chinese mainland. Nevertheless, China claims all of the Spratly Islands as its domain because of a brief period centuries ago when its navy had control of the area. Heated disagreements over who owns all or part of the Spratlys continue to fester. The Philippine government has stymied Chinese expansion on Mischief Reef by firing on Chinese vessels in the area and seeking U.S. assistance in increasing the Philippines naval and air forces in the South China Sea.

Despite the often ambivalent relationship between the United States and the Philippines and the latter's unsettling cycle of corruption and revolution, there are three main reasons—aside from the possibility of oil near the Philippines' shores—why the United States is interested in aiding its former colony. First, the Philippines shares democratic ideals with the United States. Despite its somewhat unorthodox approach by Western standards, the Philippines is a working democracy in an area not known for democratic traditions. Second, because of security issues such as terrorist strongholds in this region of the world, it behooves the U.S. military to rekindle its friendship with its Filipino allies. The Philippine

government has publicly expressed its alliance with the United States in the fight against global terrorism. The partnership, Macapagal-Arroyo has stated, is anchored in the two countries' common belief in strong democratic institutions. Third, there are over 2 million Americans of Filipino descent in the United States and over a hundred thousand American citizens in the Philippines. The result is a steady flow of tourists, family members, scholars, artists, and businesspeople between the two countries. This is a symbiotic relationship that benefits the economy of both countries.

President George Bush meets with President Gloria Macapagal-Arroyo. The United States and the Philippines enjoy a partnership that benefits the economy of both nations.

TOURISM

It is not just Americans and Filipino Americans who want to come to the Philippines. Many people are drawn to the Philippines, despite its thorny problems. In a country once described as the "Pearl of the Orient," tourism may be the real jewel that sparks the economy and brings the Philippines into its own as a flourishing modern nation. The Filipino people have earned a reputation for warmly welcoming visitors. Those who come to Manila experience a city with international flair and flavor. In the countryside as well, the islands offer fascinating combinations of Asian, Spanish, and American cultures. The country's tropical climate, other than in rainy seasons, is close to perfect, and so are its countless white-sand beaches.

As a nature lover's paradise, the island of Palawan is unparalleled in the number of endemic species of birds and animals it sustains. Vast underwater caves, remote mountain ranges, and spectacular coral reefs have turned many other islands into meccas for adventure seekers. Apo Reef off the west coast of Mindoro and the Tubbataha Reefs in the Sulu Sea, near Palawan, are two of the world's best diving spots.

If this beautiful country is to attract more tourists and investors, however, the agenda for achieving a better tomorrow must be a comprehensive one: to circumvent nature, protect the environment while accelerating economic growth, promote peaceful regional and national reconciliation, and restore confidence in government. Some progress toward these goals has been made. The effects of natural disasters, while they cannot be eliminated, are being lessened by better ways to predict and prepare for them. New strains of high-yield rice and other staples are reducing the devastating effects of droughts and floods. Environmental protections are being enforced. The Philippines has renewed negotiations with MNLF and MILF leaders and strengthened ties with allies in Asia and the United States. It is hoped that such conciliatory efforts will reduce dissent and curb terrorism as well as revitalize and stabilize the economy. In the continuing search for stability, however, whoever leads the Philippines must do so by example if the country is to be free of its hard-to-shake reputation as a corrupt political culture.

Certainly, Filipinos have time and again demonstrated that they are a resilient people capable of adapting to change and calamity. But at the heart of their national struggle lies a difficult problem even for the most indefatigable people to overcome: poverty. Drastically reducing the number of people who are desperately poor remains the greatest challenge the country faces. In 2002, the president asked all citizens, despite the disagreements they may have with one another, to join her in a new, peaceful, people's revolution—one against poverty.

There are indications that the war is slowly being won. The Philippine government reports the economy grew 5.6 percent in the first quarter of 2003, exceeding expectations. President Macapagal-Arroya has earmarked billions of pesos for economic development programs in rural regions. Aid from the U.S. Agency for International Development, at $84 million in 2003, is supporting the Arroyo administration's war on poverty as well as the peaceful resolution of conflicts in Mindanao and a zero-tolerance policy for political corruption. Most encouraging of all, the Philippine government's June 2003 economic indicators show poverty dropping to its lowest level in sixteen years.

Facts About Philippines

Government

Formal name: Republic of the Philippines

Type: Republic

Capital: Manila

Administrative divisions: 17 regions, 115 cities

Constitution: February 11, 1987

Suffrage: Universal, but not compulsory, at age 18

Executive branch: *chief of state:* President Gloria Macapagal-Arroyo (since January 20, 2001) and Vice President Teofisto Guingona (since January 20, 2001); note—the president is both the chief of state and head of government; *cabinet:* cabinet appointed by the president; *elections:* president and vice president elected on separate tickets by popular vote for six-year terms; election last held May 11, 1998 (next to be held May 16, 2004)

Legislative branch: bicameral congress consists of the Senate (24 seats; one-half elected every three years; members elected by popular vote to serve six-year terms) and the House of Representatives (214 seats; members elected by popular vote to serve three-year terms); *elections:* Senate—last held May 14, 2001 (next to be held May 16, 2004); House of Representatives—last held May 14, 2001 (next to be held May 16, 2004)

Judicial branch: Supreme Court justices are appointed by the president and serve until seventy years of age

Political parties: Kilusang Bagong Lipunan (New Society Movement); Laban Ng Demokratikong Pilipino (Struggle of Filipino Democrats) or LDP; Lakas; Liberal Party or LP; Nacionalista Party; National People's Coalition or NPC; PDP-Laban; People's Reform Party or PRP

Independence: July 4, 1946 (from the United States)

National flag: two equal horizontal bands of blue (top) and red with a white equilateral triangle based on the hoist side; in the center of the triangle is a yellow sun with eight primary rays (each containing three individual rays) and in each corner of the triangle is a small yellow five-pointed star

NATIONAL HOLIDAYS

January 1: New Year's Day

February 24: ESDA Revolution Day

Usually April: Maundy Thursday, Good Friday in Easter week

April 9: Day of Valor, commemorating bravery of Filipino soldiers who fought in World War II

May 1: Labor Day, in honor of Filipino workers

June 12: Independence Day (1898, from Spain)

Last Sunday in August: National Heroes Day

November 1: All Saints' Day

November 30: Bonifacio Day

December 25: Christmas Day

December 30: Rizal Day

PEOPLE

Nationality: Filipino

Ethnic groups: Christian Malay, 91.5 percent; Muslim Malay, 4 percent; Chinese, 1.5 percent; other, 3 percent

Population (2002): 84.6 million

Population growth (2002): 1.99 percent

Fertility rate (2002): 3.35 children born per woman

Birth rate (2002): 26.88 births per 1,000 population

Death rate (2002): 5.95 deaths per 1,000 population

Life expectancy (2002): total population, 68.12 years; female, 71.12 years; male, 65.26 years

Infant mortality rate (2002): 27.87 deaths per 1,000 live births

Religion: Roman Catholic, 83 percent; Protestant, 9 percent; Muslim, 5 percent; Buddhist and other, 3 percent

Languages: Pilipino (based on Tagalog), national language; English, language of government and instruction in higher education

Education: Years compulsory, 6; attendance, above 97 percent in elementary grades, 55 percent in secondary grades

Literacy rate: 94.6 percent

Percent of population below poverty line (2001): 40 percent

GEOGRAPHY

Location: Southeast Asia, archipelago between the Philippine Sea and the South China Sea, east of Vietnam; geographic coordinates: 13 00 N, 122 00 E; stretches for about 1,150 miles north to south

Major island groups: Luzon, the Visayas, Mindanao

Area: about 115,000 square miles (300,000 square kilometers)

Coastline: 22,550 miles (36,289 kilometers)

Highest point: Mount Apo (9,692 feet, 2,954 meters)

Terrain: 7,107 islands; 65 percent mountainous, with narrow to extensive coastal lowlands

Natural resources: Timber, copper, nickel, iron, cobalt, silver, gold

Major rivers: On Luzon, Cagayan, Pampanga, and Agno; on Mindanao, Agusan and Pulangi (Rio Grande). The Pasig River, although short, is strategic because Manila is situated at its mouth.

Mountain ranges: Sierra Madre and Cordillera Central, both on Luzon

CLIMATE

Tropical, with abundant rainfall. Weather patterns are complex, but generally, three seasons: rainy from June to October (summer monsoon season), cool and dry from November to February, and hot and dry from March to May.

Temperatures: from 70 degrees F to 90 degrees F with an 81 degree F average (in Manila)

ECONOMY

Note: All monetary figures are in U.S. dollars. Most figures are estimates.

Currency: Philippine peso (PHP)

Exchange rate (January 2002): Philippine pesos per U.S. dollar—51.2

Import commodities: raw materials, capital goods, consumer goods, fuels

ARMED FORCES

Defense spending (1998): $995 million

Defense spending as percent of GDP (1998): 1.5 percent

Military branches: army, navy (including coast guard and marine corps), air force, paramilitary units

Age for military service (2002): 20 years

NOTES

CHAPTER 1: ISLAND GEMS ON A RING OF FIRE

1. *Volcano World*, "Tectonics and Volcanoes of the Philippines." http://volcano.und.edu.

2. Quoted in *Taal—A Decade Volcano*, "History of Taal's Activity to 1911 as Described by Fr. Saderra Maso." www.iml.rwth-aachen.de.

3. Mary Somers Heidhues, *Southeast Asia: A Concise History.* London: Thames & Hudson, 2000, p. 113.

CHAPTER 2: A NATION OF DIVERSE ISLAND DWELLERS

4. Chester L. Hunt, "The Society and Its Environment," in Ronald E. Dolan, ed., *The Philippines: A Country Study.* Washington, DC: Library of Congress, Federal Research Division, 1993, p. 76.

5. Paul Rodell, *Culture and Customs of the Philippines.* Westport, CT: Greenwood, 2002, p. 6.

6. Rodell, *Culture and Customs of the Philippines*, p. 7.

7. Maria V. Staniukovich, "Peacemaking Ideology in a Headhunting Society," in Peter P. Schweitzer, Megan Biesele, and Robert K. Hitchcock, eds., *Hunters & Gatherers in the Modern World: Conflict, Resistance, and Self-Determination.* New York: Berghahn Books, 2000, p. 400.

8. Francis Dorai, ed., *Insight Guide: Philippines.* New York: APA, 2002, p. 56.

9. H. Arlo Nimmo, *The Sea People of Sulu: A Study of Social Change in the Philippines.* San Francisco: Chandler, 1972, p. 11.

10. B.R. Rodil, *The Lumad and Moro of Mindanao.* London: Manchester Free Press, 1993, p. 25.

CHAPTER 3: THE FIGHT FOR FREEDOM

11. Rodell, *Culture and Customs of the Philippines*, pp. 11–12.

12. Rodell, *Culture and Customs of the Philippines*, p. 12.

13. *America's Boy: A Century of Colonialism in the Philippines.* New York: Henry Holt, 1998, p. 28.

14. Donald Seekins, "Historical Setting," in Dolan, *The Philippines*, p. 25.

15. Seekins, "Historical Setting," p. 43.

16. Rodell, *Culture and Customs of the Philippines*, p. 20.

17. Rodell, *Culture and Customs of the Philippines*, p. 23.

CHAPTER 4: A MODERN NATION EMERGES

18. Rodell, *Culture and Customs of the Philippines*, p. 26.

19. Quoted in Republic of the Philippines Official Website, "Office of the President." www.gov.ph.

20. Rodell, *Culture and Customs of the Philippines*, p. 206.

21. Hunt, "The Society and Its Environment," p. 95.

CHAPTER 5: A VIBRANT CULTURE

22. Quoted in Thelma B. Kintanar and Sylvia Mendez Ventura, *Self-Portraits: Twelve Filipina Artists Speak.* Manila: Ateneo de Manila University Press, 1999, p. 187.

23. Rodell, *Culture and Customs of the Philippines*, p. 69.

CHAPTER 6: THE SEARCH FOR STABILITY

24. U.S. Senate Committee on Foreign Relations, *The Philippines: Present Political Status and Its Role in the New Asia. Hearing Before the Subcommittee on East Asian and Pacific Affairs of the Committee on Foreign Relations of the United States Senate*, 107th Cong., 1st sess. March 6, 2001, p. 27. www.access.gpo.gov.

25. Charles W. Lindsey, "The Economy," in Dolan, *The Philippines*, pp. 151–52.

26. Philippine European Solidarity Centre (PESC-KSP), "A Statement of Concern on the Mining Act of 1995, February 28, 1998." www philsol.nl.

Chronology

A.D. 900–1200
Chinese establish trading posts along coasts.

1400
Muslim clergy from Malaya bring Islam to the Philippines.

1521
Spaniard Ferdinand Magellan lands on Cebu and claims the land for Spain. Local chief Lapu Lapu slays Magellan on nearby island of Mactan. The Spanish expedition leaves.

1565
An expedition headed by Miguel López de Legazpi successfully establishes settlement for Spain on Cebu.

1571
Legazpi moves his headquarters to Manila, declares it the capital, and orders construction of the Intramuros. The Spanish begin to colonize the country.

1872
The Spanish execute three Filipino priests after an uprising south of Manila in Cavite. Nationalist sentiments take root.

1892
José Rizal founds La Liga Filipina; Andres Bonifacio founds the Katipunan.

1896
Colonists imprison and murder hundreds of Filipinos in Manila. Bonifacio and Katipunan rebels launch the Philippine Revolution. Emilio Aguinaldo and rebel troops capture Cavite. The Spanish execute Rizal.

1898
On June 12, Emilio Aguinaldo declares the Philippines independent from Spain and proclaims himself president. After ruling for 333 years, the Spaniards leave. The United

States and Spain go to war over rights to Cuba. In the Philippines, the United States defeats Spain with help of Filipino forces. In the Treaty of Paris, Spain grants United States authority over the Philippines. American rule begins, lasting for forty-eight years.

1899
Another war breaks out, this time between the United States and the Philippines. Aguinaldo is inaugurated as president of the first Philippine republic.

1916
The U.S. Congress authorizes phasing in of independence for Philippines.

1935
Manuel Quezon is elected president and the Philippines is declared an American commonwealth. Independence is promised for 1945.

1941
The Japanese attack Pearl Harbor, and World War II interrupts the plan for independence. The Japanese land on Luzon.

1942
The Japanese capture Manila. U.S. general Douglas MacArthur, who is in charge of Allied troops defending the Philippines, flees to Australia, promising, "I shall return." The Hukbalahap is established.

1943
The Japanese install a puppet republic, naming José Laurel as president. There are brutal consequences for those who oppose Japanese rule. Many members of the Filipino elite outwardly support the Japanese.

1944
Quezon dies in exile. MacArthur does return and launches an Allied campaign to retake the Philippines.

1945
The Allies recapture Manila, but many buildings are destroyed in bombings.

1946
Manuel Roxas is elected president. The United States grants Filipinos their independence on July 4.

1951
The United States and the Philippines sign a mutual defense treaty.

1965
Ferdinand Marcos defeats Diosdado Macapagal in his bid for reelection.

1969
Marcos becomes first Filipino president to be reelected.

1972
Marcos institutes martial law. He and his wife, Imelda, who have amassed a huge fortune, are accused of government fraud and corruption.

1981
Marcos ends martial law but declares himself the winner in a hotly contested reelection.

1983
Popular opposition candidate Benigno Aquino, returning from exile in the United States, is assassinated on arrival at Manila airport. The Marcos government denies involvement, further inflaming the populace. The economic crisis continues.

1986
Marcos, expecting little opposition, stages a "snap election," running against Corazon Aquino, the widow of Benigno Aquino. Aquino receives a majority of electoral votes, but Marcos declares himself the winner. Millions rise up in protest in the four-day People Power revolution. Aquino is inaugurated; the Marcoses flee the country. A series of coups backed by Marcos supporters begins.

1987
A new constitution is ratified. The ceasefire with New People's Army ends, and attempted coups continue. The economy weakens further.

1988

The United States agrees to pay the Aquino government for use of military bases in the Philippines. Nationalists fear the move may foster dysfunctional dependence on the United States.

1991

A debate on the merits of having American military bases in the Philippines is interrupted by an eruption of Mount Pinatubo. The United States closes down its bases in the Philippines.

1992

Fidel Ramos, a strong ally of Aquino and her defense secretary, wins the presidential election. Ramos introduces numerous reforms and opens negotiations with Muslim insurgents in the southern islands. Encouraged by his competence, foreigners invest in the Philippines. Asian financial crisis offsets some of the economic gains Ramos achieves.

1998

Action movie star Joseph Estrada, billing himself as a man of the people, is elected.

2000

Impeachment proceedings begin against Estrada, who is accused of corruption and fraud. The economy withers.

2001

The impeachment fails on technicalities, and citizen protests again gel into the People Power Revolution. The Philippine military withdraws support for Estrada. Gloria Macapagal-Arroyo, his vice president and the daughter of Diosdado Macapagal, takes over the government.

2003

Terrorist attacks escalate. Nevertheless, on political, social, and economic fronts, cautious optimism prevails.

FOR FURTHER READING

BOOKS

Howard Chua-Eoan, *Corazon Aquino.* World Leaders Past & Present series. New York: Chelsea House, 1988. For readers who are interested in learning more about the woman behind the People Power Revolution, this biography presents a detailed look at the life of Corazon Aquino and her remarkable metamorphosis from Filipino housewife to president of the Philippines.

Joaquin L. Gonzalez, *Philippines.* Countries of the World series. Milwaukee: Gareth Stevens, 2001. Up-to-date information on the geography, history, government, and culture of the Philippines.

Gordy Slack, *Ferdinand Marcos.* World Leaders Past & Present series. New York: Chelsea House, 1988. This biography examines the rise to power of one of the most controversial leaders in Philippine history.

Lily Rose R. Tope, *Philippines.* Cultures of the World series. New York: Marshall Cavendish, 1991. Although it covers presidential politics only through the Corazon Aquino years, this book presents good general information on Philippine history and culture.

WEBSITES

Indo-Malayan Philippines, World Wildlife Foundation (www.panda.org). This site divides the Philippines into ecoregions and provides detailed information on such concerns as endangered species and deforestation.

Philippines, The World Factbook 2002 (www.odci.gov). Prepared by the Central Intelligence Agency, this site provides the latest available statistics on the country in categories such as economy, transportation, communication, and government.

Volcano World (http://volcano.und.edu). A kid-friendly website with a wealth of information on the world's volcanoes, including more than one dozen in the Philippines. Volcano World was originally funded by National Aeronautics and Space Administration and hosted by scientists at the University of North Dakota.

Works Consulted

Books

Reynaldo G. Alejandro, ed., *The Food of the Philippines.* Boston: Periplus Editions, 1998. A way to sample the culture through the cuisine.

Raymond Bonner, *Waltzing with a Dictator: The Marcoses and the Making of American Policy.* New York: Times Books, 1987. A popular account of U.S.-Philippine relations during the Marcos years.

John Bresnan, ed., *Crisis in the Philippines: The Marcos Era and Beyond.* Princeton, NJ: Princeton University Press, 1986. A scholarly examination of the implications of Ferdinand Marcos's policies.

Harry S. Calit, ed., *The Philippines: Current Issues and Historical Background.* Hauppauge, NY: Nova Science, 2003. The articles on terrorism and security provide the latest available information on these subjects.

Ronald E. Dolan, ed, *The Philippines: A Country Study.* Washington, DC: Library of Congress, Federal Research Division, 1993. This book provides scholarly insights on Philippine history, society, economy, and politics through June 1991.

Francis Dorai, ed., *Insight Guide: Philippines.* New York: APA, 2002. Although intended as a travel guide, this book contains informative special features on Filipino culture, a concise history, and detailed information on regions.

Luis Francia, ed., *Brown River, White Ocean: An Anthology of Twentieth-Century Philippine Literature in English.* Piscataway, NJ: Rutgers University Press, 1993. An insightful anthology of writings by Filipinos and Filipino Americans from the 1900s to the 1990s. It includes stories and poems by such renowned writers as Carlos Bulosan and José Garcia Villa.

James Hamilton-Paterson, *America's Boy: A Century of Colonialism in the Philippines.* New York: Henry Holt, 1998. This book focuses on the career of Ferdinand Marcos, but it also provides vignettes of Filipino village life and background information on events leading up to Marcos's scandalous reign.

Barbara Joan Hansen, *Barbara Hansen's Taste of Southeast Asia: Brunei, Indonesia, Malaysia, the Philippines, Singapore, Thailand & Vietnam.* Tucson, AZ: HPBooks, 1987. For the adventuresome cook, this book provides an entertaining way to compare the dishes of the Pacific region.

Mary Somers Heidhues, *Southeast Asia: A Concise History.* London: Thames & Hudson, 2000.

Thelma B. Kintanar and Sylvia Mendez Ventura, *Self-Portraits: Twelve Filipina Artists Speak.* Manila: Ateneo de Manila University Press, 1999. Biographies of and candid interviews with contemporary women in the arts. Reproductions of many of their works are included.

A.L. Kroeber, *Peoples of the Philippines.* Westport, CT: Greenwood, 1974. A classic work written by a professor of anthropology at the University of California.

Walter A. McDougall, *Let the Sea Make a Noise: A History of the North Pacific from Magellan to MacArthur.* New York. BasicBooks, 1993. This lengthy history covers the rise and fall of empires in the Asia Pacific region from the sixteenth to twentieth century in great detail. It is written by a Pulitzer Prize–winning historian who knows how to make facts read like an adventure novel.

H. Arlo Nimmo, *The Sea People of Sulu: A Study of Social Change in the Philippines.* San Francisco: Chandler, 1972. This study offers a detailed analysis of the changes that have occurred among the elusive Bajau of the Sulu Archipelago.

Robert H. Reid and Eileen Guerrero, *Corazon Aquino and the Brushfire Revolution.* Baton Rouge: Louisiana State University Press, 1995. This is an in-depth look at the personality and presidency of Corazon Aquino.

Paul Rodell, *Culture and Customs of the Philippines.* Westport, CT: Greenwood, 2002. An excellent overview of the history and culture of the archipelago.

B.R. Rodil, *The Lumad and Moro of Mindanao.* London: Manchester Free Press, 1993. This book presents the point of view of two of the Philippines' ethnic groups.

Daniel B. Schirmer and Stephen Rosskamm Shalom, eds., *The Philippines Reader: A History of Colonialism, Neo-colonialism, Dictatorship, and Resistance.* Boston: South End, 1987. This is a collection of articles and documents on the Philippines' struggle for independence from the 1900s to the presidency of Corazon Aquino.

Peter P. Schweitzer, Megan Biesele, and Robert K. Hitchcock, eds., *Hunters & Gatherers in the Modern World: Conflict, Resistance, and Self-Determination.* New York: Berghahn Books, 2000. One essay dispels stereotypes about the elusive Ifuago.

Southeast Asia. Alexandria, VA: Time-Life Books, 1987. Chapter five covers Philippine history and society.

Leslie E. Sponsel, ed., *Endangered Peoples of Southeast & East Asia.* Westport, CT: Greenwood, 2000. James Eder writes about the Batak in great depth in this collection of studies.

David Joel Steinberg, *The Philippines: A Singular and a Plural Place.* 4th ed. Boulder, CO: Westview, 2000. This latest version of the book covers Philippine society and politics through the Estrada years. The first edition was endorsed by Benigno Aquino Jr. as "must reading" for anyone seeking a true understanding of the Philippines.

Edgar Wickberg, *The Chinese in Philippine Life, 1850–98.* New Haven, CT: Yale University Press, 1965. A definitive work on the Chinese during this era.

INTERNET SOURCES

Philippine European Solidarity Centre (PESC-KSP), "A Statement of Concern on the Mining Act of 1995, February 28, 1998." www.philsol.n1.

Taal—A Decade Volcano, "History of Taal's Activity to 1911 as Described by Fr. Saderra Maso." www.iml.rwth-aachen.de.

U.S. Senate Committee on Foreign Relations, *The Philippines: Present Political Status and Its Role in the New Asia. Hearing Before the Subcommittee on East Asian and Pacific Affairs of the Committee on Foreign Relations of the United States Senate*, 107th Cong., 1st sess., March 6, 2001. www. gpo.access.gov.

Volcano World, "Tectonics and Volcanoes of the Philippines." http://volcano.und.edu.

PERIODICALS

Newsweek, "People Power II," January 29, 2001.

Time, "Another Thrilla in Manila: Tired of Corruption, the Philippine People Eject a Once Popular President," January 29, 2001.

VIDEOS

Fire on the Rim. New York: Ambrose Video Publishing. 1990. Fantastic four-volume series on the Pacific Rim produced by PBS. Ties together scientific information on earthquakes and volcanoes with folktales various peoples have developed to explain and cope with natural disasters. Episode 1: *Fire into Gold;* Episode 2: *Stories from the Earth;* Episode 3: *The Prediction Problem;* Episode 4: *Preparing for Disaster.*

WEBSITES

"Fire and Mud: Eruptions and Lahars of Mount Pinatubo, Philippines," **U.S. Geological Survey** (http://pubs.usgs. gov). This website provides a wealth of information on the 1991 eruption of Mount Pinatubo from a scientific point of view and includes a number of dramatic photographs.

Chris Newhall, James W. Hendley II, and Peter H. Stauffer, "Benefits of Volcano Monitoring Far Outweigh Costs— The Case of Mount Pinatubo," **U.S. Geological Survey** (http://wrgis.wr.usgs.gov). This is a detailed fact sheet produced by USGS that provides numerous links to other Pinatubo-related research and reports.

Republic of the Philippines Official Website (www.gov.ph). This site provides a great deal of useful information on all aspects of Filipino society and gives the latest news from the president's office.

Riceworld, "Mountains of Rice, Beauty & Toil" (www.rice world.org). This portion of the website features photographs and comments on the Banuae rice terraces: Riceworld is sponsored by the International Rice Research Institute.

Pinatubo Volcano "The Sleeping Giant Awakens" (http:// park.org/philippines). This website contains a history, glossary, and facts about Mount Pinatubo.

Taal—A Decade Volcano (www.iml.rwth-aachen.de). This site contains historical and current information about this well-known Philippine volcano.

U.S. Department of State, "Background Notes: Philippines" (www.state.gov). This website is an excellent source of concise information on the Philippines. Updated October 2000.

Index

PICTURE CREDITS

ABOUT THE AUTHOR

Writer and editor Mary Campbell Wild has a bachelor's degree in English from Chestnut Hill College in Philadelphia and a master's degree in international communication from American University in Washington, D.C. Over a twenty-five year career, she has written numerous feature articles and contributed to federal aerospace- and defense-related documents; university-based studies of European, African, and Asian nations; and scientific and medical journals. This is her first book. Wild lives with her husband and son in Takoma Park, Maryland.